Perspectives on National Integration

Perspectives on National Integration

A Trilingual Book

English • Hindi • Urdu

Editors

Mirza Asmer Beg

Abdur Raheem Kidwai

Viva Books

New Delhi | Mumbai | Chennai | Kolkata | Bengaluru | Hyderabad | Kochi | Guwahati

Publisher's note

First Published 2013

Viva Books Private Limited

- 4737/23, Ansari Road, Daryaganj, New Delhi 110 002
  Tel. 42242200, 23258325, 23283121, Email: vivadelhi@vivagroupindia.net
- 76, Service Industries, Shirvane, Sector 1, Nerul, Navi Mumbai 400 706
  Tel. 27721273, 27721274, Email: vivamumbai@vivagroupindia.net
- Jamals Fazal Chambers, 26 Greams Road, Chennai 600 006
  Tel. 28294241, 28290304, Email: vivachennai@vivagroupindia.net
- B-103, Jindal Towers, 21/1A/3 Darga Road, Kolkata 700 017
  Tel. 22816713, Email: vivakolkata@vivagroupindia.net
- 7, GF, Sovereign Park Aptts., 56-58, K. R. Road, Basavanagudi, Bengaluru 560 004
  Tel. 26607409, Email: vivabangalore@vivagroupindia.net
- 101-102, Moghal Marc Apartments, 3-4-637 to 641, Narayanguda, Hyderabad 500 029
  Tel. 27564481, Email: vivahyderabad@vivagroupindia.net
- First Floor, Beevi Towers, SRM Road, Kaloor, Kochi 682 018
  Tel. 0484-2403055, 2403056, Email: vivakochi@vivagroupindia.net
- 232, GNB Road, Beside UCO Bank, Silpukhuri, Guwahati 781 003
  Tel. 0361-2666386, Email: vivaguwahati@vivagroupindia.net

www.vivagroupindia.com

ISBN: 978-81-309-2274-4

Published by Vinod Vasishtha for Viva Books Private Limited, 4737/23 Ansari Road, Daryaganj, New Delhi 110 002.

Printed and bound by Raj Press, R-3, Inderpuri, New Delhi 110 012.

S0000

Contents

URDU

Introduction

India is a country of rich cultural heritage with diversities of religion, language, caste, class and region. Our unique historical backdrop, which was characterized by the presence of diverse identities – social, regional, linguistic and cultural, required that a key role be given to the state through which the composite nation was to be created. The state was at once a symbol of authority and an instrument of social change. For long the nation-building process was conceived to be one that concomitantly led to greater unity of the nation and greater involvement and participation for the citizen in the institutions of the state. This led to the understanding that democratic participation was the best way of achieving national integration. Hence, the project to promote democracy through the very composition and institutional structures of the state was started. Implicit in the Westminster model, which we adopted, was a conception with two ostensibly opposite ideas but which were meant to serve a common purpose. The first of these was to make the new state encompass diverse interests and identities; the second was to assign primacy to the state in the whole process of nation- building. Embedded in the first is a decentralized conception of sharing power and carrying diverse entities in a common project. The second, on the other hand, in due course could produce a centralized model of governance. But the two together were meant to produce a practicable balance between a strong and consistent centre and a series of living sub-centers representing the large variety of structures and spaces through which a composite nation state was to actualize. The nationalist ideology that had accompanied such a conception was both integrative and open to diverse interests and groupings, including dissenting ones.

With the passage of time, this form of a nation state is increasingly being questioned. On the one hand, the state is ceasing to be the central mechanism of the nation, while on the other hand the 'nation' that had come into being has entered a process of severe disintegration, multiple polarizations and likely collapse. Both the retreat of the state and the erosion of the nation are going side by side, one being hijacked by the global 'order' and 'market' and the other facing serious challenges from within, from different regions and nationalities. With this the project of nation-building is facing a lot of obstacles.

We are today facing increasing disparities in incomes. On the one hand a small minority is getting stinking rich, on the other hand, majority of Indians are finding it difficult to make both ends meet. This mounting gap between the rich and poor provides an ideal ground for the growth of despicable tendencies like naxalism, terrorism and crime, which threaten the very existence of our nation-state. Different regions and nationalities, are seen to be increasingly demanding, mostly not motivated by a desire to dominate, but by a fear of being subjugated and marginalized. The challenge which continues to stare us in the face is that our national/Indian identity, which should have been primary, is obscured by other identities of community, caste, class, region and language. Since our parochial identities are often primary for us, when we act in the public sphere, our actions are conditioned by these identities. Hence, rather than acting as an Indian, we act as a Hindu/Muslim, or upper/lower caste person or are guided by some other such narrow identity. Unless we reach a point where, every Indian considers himself an Indian first, the integration of India will remain incomplete.

What is required here is not the forcible dilution of all differences, but an effort towards forging unity in diversity. We require integration, not assimilation. For actualizing this national goal, the significance of the grand project of national integration becomes even more fundamental.

It was against this backdrop that we decided to bring out this volume, which has basically tried to look at this important issue from different perspectives.

In his paper, A.K. Verma argues that national integration is usually taken as synonymous with communal harmony. This paper takes a different trajectory and argues that casteism is no less a threat to national integration than communalism. There are caste divisions and dissensions within each religious community that are no less detrimental to the social fabric than the communal disharmony. The communal angle to national integration divides Indian society into two broad meta-religious identities viz. Hindus and Muslims, but, the caste angle transcends these meta-religious identities and looks at the several micro-identities of which the religious meta-identities are made of. Castes and casteism are not confined to Hindus alone; Muslims, Christians and Sikhs too are neck deep into it. While the philosophy of various religions may be egalitarian and humanitarian, but the evolution of various religions in India has given them a unique social flavour. The hierarchical nature of Indian society has crept into all major religions, and hence there are lots of discriminations and conflicts within various social groups composing a religious denomination. Casteism harms religious homogenisation within a religious community, breeds 'internal exclusions' detrimental to minorities in a religious community, prevents subaltern class formation, and subsumes gender into caste preventing formation of a women class – consequences that go against the basic requirements of national integration.

K.C. Sreekumar has viewed national integration as a process and project carried out by a political system to foster nationalism among its people. His paper looks at the limitations of the old concept of the nation-state and the multi-ethnic nature of the modern State. Conflict is inherent in a plural society. So there is a need for resolving such conflicts with the aim of generating consensus. Conflict resolution by adopting accommodative techniques is preferable to that of assimilation. This would help the process of national integration in a plural society. In the case of India we have adopted such an approach after Independence. This is made clear by a study of three major problems faced by the country such as, the demand for States reorganization, the Assam problem and the Punjab problem. The task of the political system was made easier by many factors such as the fundamental unity of India, the vibrant nature of her democracy, the fast growing economy, the vision of her political leadership, the adoption of a successful education system, and the introduction of modern ICT. A deep awareness about the manner in which national integration is brought about in this country so far would definitely enable future policy makers to further strengthen the integrity of the nation.

In his paper, Sanjeer Alam maintains that since independence, India has accorded high priority to the concerns of national integration. While the sources of disintegrative forces in a geographically and socially diverse country are many and complex, the presence of minority groups based on ethnicity, language, religion and so on is, nonetheless, seen as a major obstacle to achieve national integration. In India, as elsewhere, the problem of national integration is generally perceived in terms of the role and aspirations of different minority groups. For historical and demographic reasons, it is basically the role of the Muslim community in the process of national development and their attitude towards the wider society around which the discourse on national integration has revolved. Traditionally, the discourse of national integration with reference to the Muslims has centered on the issues typically associated with their religious and cultural identity. A widespread feeling has existed all along that Muslims are overly sensitive to their distinctive socio-cultural ethos. They are so obsessed with their religion and socio-cultural ethos that the treatment of these issues by the state, in their view, reflects actual treatment of them. This paper, however, argues that the issues relating to religio-cultural identity may not concern all Muslims. The formidable barrier to their integration is their persistent exclusion from the structures of social, economic and political opportunities. As social integration precedes national integration, social integration of minorities is difficult to achieve unless they are able or enabled to fully participate in the activities of wider society. Seen in this context, the conventional discourse on national integration with reference to the role of minorities is not only narrow in its construct but also problematic. Therefore, there is a need for re-orienting/restructuring the conventional discourse on national integration so as to focus on the problems of 'exclusion' and strategy for 'inclusion' of the Muslims in the wider structures of opportunities.

Mirza Asmer Beg argues that in India there is no unanimity in the understanding of the term 'national integration', however, we need to understand it against the backdrop of the context in which it evolved. He discusses the various challenges which the process of national integration in India has to surmount and the problems which we continue to encounter in this course. He also highlights the positive developments as regards nation-building in India and how we need to maximize the benefits from these advances.

S. Imtiaz Hasnain maintains that India as a nation-state has several kinds or diversities, including language. Hence it becomes important for the government to have strategies for national integration, which allow linguistic diversity. He adds that the constitution of India provides adequate safeguards for presenting linguistic and cultural identities. He also highlights the multiplicity of race, religion, language and script in India and Indian multilingualism.

Dr. S. Reshma Jamal has studied the 15 Orientation Programmes which were successfully conducted by the UGC Academic Staff College, AMU in the four years i.e. 2006–07, 2007–08 2008–09 and 2009–10. In these training programmes 539 participants were enrolled. The written assignments on

National Integration submitted by Orientation Programme participants of the last four years have been analysed. The level of enrichment on the issue is assessed by the language and content delivered. The data were collected on a scale of low and high vis-a-vis National Integration. The Participants opinions have been analysed.

A part from the general readership, this volume is addressed in particular to the participants of the UGC Academic Staff College Orientation Programme. As part of our years long association with the UGC Academic Staff College, Aligarh Muslim University, Aligarh, we found these thousands of course participant, who happen to be the University/College teachers drawn from all parts of the country very receptive to the discussions and presentations on the theme of National Integration. Needless to add, such sensitization is essential for the well being of our polity. We are sure the readers will find this volume enlightening, inspiring and engaging.

August 2012
Aligarh Muslim Univerity
Aligarh

Mirza Asmer Beg
A.R. Kidwai

About the Contributors

Dr. Mohd. Sanjeer Alam is trained in social geography and social demography at the Centre for the Study of Regional Development (CSRD), Jawaharlal Nehru University, Delhi, from where he received his Ph.D in 2005. Currently, he is Visiting Associate Fellow at Centre for the Study of Developing Societies (CSDS), Delhi. Sanjeer Alam has researched extensively on socio-spatial inequalities in accessing publicly provided goods and services with particular focus on disadvantaged groups, including the Muslim minorities. Alam's work has been published in reputed academic and professional journals and his book – Religion, Community and Education: The Case of Rural Bihar (Oxford University Press, Delhi) – is forthcoming.

Dr. A.K. Verma is Chair, Political Science Department, Christ Church College, Kanpur. His current research interest focuses on Electoral Studies in Uttar Pradesh. He was invited by Harvard University, California University, Berkeley, State University of New York, Stony Brooks, Australian National University, IIT-Kanpur and several Indian Universities to explain his theories of 'Social Osmosis' and 'Reverse Social Osmosis' that offer a rationale for the rise of exclusionary politics and transition from exclusionary to inclusive politics in Uttar Pradesh. Dr. Verma has published many research papers published in refereed journals. He has edited several journals. Currently, he is editor of Shodharthy. He was a Member of Textbook Development Team, NCERT, Delhi for the preparation of the New Generation of Text Books for Political Science under the National Curriculum Framework-2005.

Professor K.C. Sreekumar took his M.A. (Political Science), M.A. (History), and Ph.D. (Pol.Sc.) from the University of Kerala. He has taught for 30 years in various N.S.S colleges, under the Calicut and Kerala Universities, and in the School of International Relations and Politics, Mahatma Gandhi University. He has served as Co-ordinator of Indira Gandhi National Open University (IGNOU), Study Centre in Thiruvananthapuram. As a National Associate of the UGC he did collaborative research in the School of Historical Studies, JNU. He has participated and presented papers in many national and international seminars. He has contributed Chapters/ Articles to more than 10 books, and edited the book: Perspectives on American Studies (Icon Publications, New Delhi, 2007). His articles have appeared in many reputed research Journals.

Professor S. Imtiaz Hasnain, Ph.D. (Jawaharlal Nehru University) is Professor of Sociolinguistics, Department of Linguistics, Aligarh Muslim University. He has published articles and books in the areas of sociolinguistics, critical discourse, language planning and minority language rights. He was a Fellow of East West Center, Hawaii, and a Senior Fellow of Central Institute of Indian Languages, Mysore. imtiaz.hasnain@gmail.com

Dr. Reeta Bagchi, Faculty of Islaimc Studies and Social Sciences, Jamia Hamdard University, New Delhi.

Dr. R.S. Varshney, Department of Sociology, S.V. College, Aligarh.

Mirza Asmer Beg is Professor of Political Science at the Aligarh Muslim University, Aligarh, India. He is Fellow of Salzburg Global Seminars, Austria. He is the author of in the *Tug-of-War*. He had contributed seven articles to the International Encyclopedia of Affirmative Action (Greenwood Publishing Company, USA). He has written more than twenty five research papers in national and international journals. He has also contributed more than fifty articles in national dailies.

Dr. S. Reshma Jamal has to her credit masters and doctorate in Psychology from the Aligarh Muslim University. She has published two books and several articles. She has been a faculty member of the UGC Academic Staff College since 2002. She coordinated several programmes on communal harmony sponsored by the National Foundation for Communal Harmony, New Delhi at the UGC Academic Staff College, AMU Aligarh.

Professor Abdulrahim P. Vijapur, Chairman, Department of Political Science, Aligarh Muslim University, Aligarh.

ENGLISH

1

Minorities and National Integration in India: Emerging Concerns and Policy Tensions

Mohd. Sanjeer Alam

Most nations, if not all, across the globe are grappled with the problem of binding various regional units and diverse people into a cohesive, well-functioning and integrated whole. However, this problem is far more formidable in the post-colonial countries with pluralistic social orders where the tensions between socio-cultural and regional identities hold back the process of nation building and national development. At times, the tensions reach such a point where even national integrity stands threatened. In view of the fact that the larger project of nation building and national development is contingent upon system stability, many post-colonial countries accord high priority to the concerns having significant bearings on 'national integration'.[1] And, India is no exception.

1. The notion of 'national integration' is inherently complex in its construct as it encompasses a wide array of interrelated cognitive, attitudinal and behavioral activities. National integration signifies both a condition and process. As a *condition*, it refers to existence of a deeper sense of belongingness to the country in which one lives and a feeling of togetherness and unity amongst different segments of population. As a *process*, national integration is the progressive lessening of ethnic, cultural and regional tensions and discontinuities in the process of creating a homogeneous political community. A distinction can, however, be made between political integration and national integration. While the former refers generally to a shifting of loyalties to the newly created centre in the system, the latter goes beyond mere co-existence of different communities. It is a socio-psychological process through which develops social cohesiveness and a sense of unity and solidarity in the hearts of the people, leading to emergence of a feeling of common citizenship and unflinching loyalty to the nation. For various definitions and perspectives on national integration also see Gani (1978) and Moin Shakir (1982).

Structurally, the population of India exhibits baffling socio-cultural diversity. One can find in it as many axes of cleavages and divisions as could be possible. Although a variety of social cleavages have existed in India through ages, they did not play themselves out on the political plane until the dawn of the British colonial power. After the colonial power was gone, the most critical question that the political leadership encountered was about managing diversities. In recognition of the fact that diversities – geographical, social and cultural – are deeply embedded in the 'idea of India' and that the best way of dealing with such diversities is to give them enough space to operate, the political leadership chose to adopt and institutionalize the strategy of 'unity in diversity'.[2]

In a geographically and socially diverse country, the sources of disintegrative forces are many and diverse. However, presence of minority groups based on ethnicity, language, religion and so on is often seen as a major problem of achieving national integration. In India, as elsewhere, the problem of national

2. The pluralistic countries facing the problem of national integration have basically adopted two kinds of strategies to achieve the goal of national integration. One is the assimilation approach that lays emphasis on assimilation of the sub-national cultures either to a particular core cultural identity or to the presumed characteristics and political affiliation of the culture of a dominant ethnic group. Indonesia can be cited as a case in point (also see Drake, 1989). The second strategy applied by the pluralistic countries lies in the philosophy of unity in diversity. This strategy involves cultivating the sense of political unity among diverse ethnic groups, while at the same time upholding and maintaining the social structures and cultural norms that make the group disparate. In other words, national integration is seen as congruence of diversities leading to a unity in which all group peculiarities are preserved rather than transforming diversity into uniformity. This strategy is adopted in many countries including India, Nigeria, Kenya and Ghana. In India, the National Integration Council constituted in 1961 declared that the foundation of our national life is common citizenship, unity in diversity, freedom of religion, secularism, equality .... and fraternity among all communities and the National Integration Council reiterates its faith in these values and dedicates itself to their achievement.

integration is generally perceived in terms of the role and aspirations of different minority groups.[3] For historical reasons,

---

3. The expression of 'minority' is generally used to refer to "a part of the population of a state that is marked off by race, or language, or religion, or some other social characteristics defined by 'ascription' (that is, a trait one carries regardless of one's behavior), which leads the people of the group to be looked on by the majority as somewhat different or 'other' and leads the minority to view the majority as both different and dominant" (Glazer 2007: 145). Structurally, the population of India is divided along multiple and overlapping axes of caste, tribe, language and religion. Each of these broad groups is spatially so unevenly distributed and within the given spatial context so internally differentiated that each sub-group of population in one context or the other stands as 'minority' group. For example, if religion as a whole is taken as the basis of defining 'minority' the followers of Islam (Muslims), Christianity, Sikhism, Jainism, Buddhism and so on are minority communities. But Muslims and Sikhs are majority communities in Jammu and Kashmir and Punjab respectively. Similarly, Christians are in majority in the states of Meghalaya, Mizoram and Nagaland. Furthermore, even as Hindus at national level constitute majority community, it is divided into hundreds of thousands sub-castes or *jatis* which not only maintain certain social distance from each other but also are often at war with each other for dominating shared social space in the given context.

The Indian Constitution, however, does not offer precise definition of the term 'minority', although it uses the word in a number of Articles (29, 30, and 350 A and 350 B). Article 29 that pertains to cultural rights of minorities states that 'any section of the citizens residing in the territory of India or any part thereof having a distinct language, script or culture of its own shall have the right to conserve the same.' Article 30 (1) mentions that 'all minorities, whether based on religion or language, shall have the right to establish and administer educational institutions of their choice'. Clearly, the Constitution of India recognizes two kinds of minorities – religious and linguistic. However, it is not clear as to what spatial unit should be taken into account for determining minority. The Supreme Court in its ruling in the case of *TMA Pai Foundation and others versus State of Karnataka and others* (2002) held that for the purpose of Article 30, a minority, whether linguistic or religious, is determinable with reference to a state and not by taking into consideration the population of the country as a whole.

The National Commission for Minorities Act (1992) states that 'minority for the purpose of the Act, means a community notified as such by the Central Government. For the purpose of the Act, the Central Government has notified the Muslim, the Christian, the Sikh, the Buddhist and the Parsi communities as 'minority communities'.

it is basically the role of the Muslim minority in the process of national development and their attitude to wider society around which the discourse on national integration has revolved. As Gani (1978: 15) points out: 'One of the great barriers to integration in India has been the highly unfavorable images the two major religious communities of India have of each other'. In this context, it would not be out of place to look at, though briefly, the historical processes that inform problems of Muslims as well as communal relations in the country.

THE MAKING OF MUSLIM MINORITY

Muslims have long been constituted, for almost over a millennia, an important element of Indian social fabric. Islam, a non-Indic religion, was first introduced to India by Arab Muslim traders who had trade relations with the people on the south – western and south – eastern coasts as early as the beginning of eighth century (A.D). In course of time, many Arab Muslim traders began to settle down instead of having mere a time bound trade relations. Many of them married to local women. The inter-marriage between the Arabs and local people gave rise to the *Moplah* Muslim community of Malabar (Qureshi 1956; Miller 1976). However, Muslims largely made inroad into India through the north-western gate. Through the north-western gate came the Turks, the Afghans and the Moghuls with hordes of their armies, conquered territories throughout the northern plains and settled in. From the eighth through eighteenth century (A.D), Islam made indelible impact on all sectors of life of the natives. One of the visible changes in the existing socio-cultural milieu that took place during this period was gradual swelling of Muslim population due to conversion of natives into Islam either voluntarily or under coercion (Qureshi 1956; Sopher 1956; Lamb 1968; Siddiqui 1976; Dutt and Devgun 1979; Ahmad

1999).[4] In course of time, the indigenous Muslims (descendents of converts from Hinduism) not only exceeded the Muslims who came across the frontiers of the Indian sub-continent but also the Hindus in many places. And yet, the Muslim community as a whole never accounted for even a quarter of total population of the sub-continent.

In due course of time, different religions created for themselves cultural niches within the shared cultural space. Muslim communities, especially those who came from outside the Indian sub-continent, integrated themselves with other sections of population at different levels of regional hierarchy (Ahmad, 1999). As a result, the Muslims like any other community developed their cultural traits expressed in terms of language, customs, dresses, dietary habits and so on under distinct regional mould.

Different religious communities lived without overt antipathy towards each other until the establishment of British rule over India. In order to get firmly rooted, the colonial power created a variety of socially differentiated identities and appropriated them

4. It has been argued that coercion played a little role, if any, in conversion. The arguments advanced to support this contention are as follows. One, bulk of those who converted to Islam belonged to lower castes Hindus who were oppressed due to their inferior position in Hindu social structure. The Sufis, the symbols of love and compassion, gave them the much needed healing touch and thereby wielded greater influence on them. This had resulted in mass conversion to Islam. Second, most of the Muslim rulers were concerned about establishing and expanding their authority across the length and breadth of the Indian sub-continent. If coercion was the main instrument of conversion, largest concentration of Muslims would have been found in the areas in or around the Muslim seats of power. But the areas of high Muslim concentration are found far away from the seats of Muslim power. Additionally, if coercion had played an important role in conversion, a large part of Indian population would have been converted to Islam under the reign of Muslim rulers for over six centuries (1175–1757). But at no point in time Muslim population exceeded a quarter of total population. Before the partition of India into two sovereign nations, Muslims accounted for about 24 per cent of total population (Census of India 1941).

for political benefits under the policy of 'divide and rule' (Metcalf 1997). However, for historical and demographic reasons, nothing would pay as much dividend to the policy of 'divide and rule' as the divide between Hindus and Muslims. The imperial power, therefore, not only heightened communal consciousness between the two communities but also effectively pitted them against each other. All this resulted in overt antipathy, mutual exclusion and contestation for greater shares in the structures of unfolding opportunities (Seal 1968; Ahmad 2004). The enmity between the two communities assumed such a position that the country had to be divided into two independent sovereign nations – India and Pakistan on 14/15 August 1947.

Even as religion combined with differing aspirations and differential access to socio-economic and power structures between Hindus and Muslims served the basis of the 'two nation theory', partition itself did not make either new nation a religiously homogeneous country. A large number of Muslims chose to stay back in India (Buultjens, 1986; Davis, 1949; 1967) and so did many Hindus in Pakistan.[5] In brief, the 'Hindu-Muslim question' remained unresolved in the subcontinent and continues to do so at present.

The formation of Pakistan as a separate country and as a homeland for Muslims created a profoundly difficult situation for those Muslims who preferred to stay back in India. For the Indian Muslims, the consequences of partition were even more adverse than at the time of collapse of the Mughal Empire. Taking into account the kind of vulnerability that the Muslim

5. As per the 1941 census, Muslims accounted for 24.2 per cent of the total population of undivided India, while Hindus were 69.5 per cent. In the 1951 Census, the Muslim population was enumerated as 9.9 per cent of India's total population, whereas Hindus accounted for about 85 per cent (Davis, 1949; Dutt and Devgun, 1979). According to the 2001 Census, Hindus account for 81 per cent of the total population, followed by Muslims (13.4 per cent), Christians and Sikhs (2 per cent each).

community would face in the post-partition situation, the early leadership of India chose to institute and to cultivate a liberal and secular state governed by a democratic constitution. But the injury that the partition itself had caused to the psyche of the Muslims and their socio-economic and political situations would not be repaired in the near future even if they were assured equal rights and privileges as given to majority community in the Constitution.

At the political level, it necessarily entailed a major diminution in their power and influence, for the partition robbed the community of articulate leadership (Gopal Krishna 1977). Added to this, their status was reduced to 'a minority acutely blamed by the Hindus for the partition of the country, a minority regarded as representative of an anti-Indian, hostile, divisive and subversive influence which had shattered the aspirations for national unity' (Murphy 1953: 124). At the social and economic level, the community was 'skimmed off' the stratum that was in the forefront of appropriating educational and economic opportunities; that produced professionals and leaders who acted as a source of inspiration for education and white-collar jobs amongst the Muslim masses and above all maintained socioeconomic and political equilibrium vis-à-vis other communities (Imam 1977; Hasan 1997). The remaining business and feudal classes suffered due to enactment of certain legislations in the aftermath of independence. The middle class that had developed the taste for joining government services in the pre-partition period was now edged out from such avenues in absence of supportive institutional arrangements such as 'reservation' during the colonial period (Husain 1965). Thus acute sense of fear, frustrations, insecurity and uncertainties – all combined to give them a narrow view of their rights as citizens. It was widely believed that the Muslims largely concerned themselves with guarding their religio-cultural identity and thus held aloof from the national mainstream.

The Problems of Muslim Minorities and National Integration

Traditionally, the problems of the Muslims that have figured out prominently in the discourse of national integration are those associated with their religious and cultural identity because these problems often boil down to communal tensions and conflict, inimical to national integration (Gani 1978). It has been repeatedly presented that Muslims are overly obsessed with their distinctive socio-cultural identity and, therefore, reluctant to respond to changing socio-economic and political conditions. They continue to share a kind of metonymic relationship with the issues of Muslim Personal Law, status of Urdu, minority status of Aligarh Muslim University and Babri Masjid such that the treatment of these issues, in their view, reflects actual treatment of them. However, there are many who have contested this narrow metric of behaviour of Muslims by arguing that neither the Muslim community itself nor its response to any of these issues has been monolithic (Gani 1978; Hasan 1989).

There is no denying the fact that the issues relating to religio-cultural identity continue to concern a large section of Muslims and are inimical to their integration into the so-called 'national mainstream'. Be that as it may, but the most formidable barrier to integration of Muslims into the national mainstream is their persistent exclusion from wider socio-economic opportunities. Many reasons could be advanced in support of this argument. In the first place, the issues related to religio-cultural identity do not exist in isolation from overall participation of the community in the structures of opportunities. A closer examination of these issues would reveal that they are actually dependent rather than independent variables.[6] Secondly, contrary to popular belief, most of the issues relating to religio-cultural identity do not have universal appeal among Muslims. For example, the problem of Urdu is basically the problem of Muslims living in north India. Similarly, not only is there diversity of opinions on the Muslim Personal Law; different sects among Muslims actually have different versions of family and inheritance laws. On the contrary, deprivation and exclusion cut across sects, linguistic and cultural groupings among Muslims and, therefore, may lead to widespread sense of alienation among them and can have dangerous implications for national integration. Thirdly and finally, social integration precedes national integration and social integration of minorities cannot be possible unless they are able to fully participate in the activities of wider society.

It thus appears that the conventional discourse on national integration with reference to the role of minorities is not only narrow in its construct but also problematic. There is, therefore, a need for re-orienting/restructuring the debate so as to focus on the problems of 'exclusion' and strategy for 'inclusion' of Muslims in the wider structures of opportunities.

6. The issues of minority status of AMU and Jamia Millia Islamia University and Urdu can be taken up for example. Needless to say that a large number of good quality institutions of higher education have come up during past six decades and yet AMU and Jamia continue to be the hub of aspiring Muslim students. It is not clear why there are few Muslim students in the country's best educational institutions, but if the two Universities for whatever reasons continue to remain the only sites of hope one can but expect arousal of huge passion in the wake of debating their minority character. It would not be erroneous to assume that if Muslim students were not dependent on the two institutions for fulfilling their educational aspirations, the issue of their minority status would not have generated so much passion and anger as it did in 1970s. Similarly, the demand for giving Urdu its legitimate place is also couched in the exclusion of educated Muslims in the avenues of employment (public or private), for the major demands for giving Urdu its due revolve round creation of employment opportunities (i.e. opening up Urdu medium educational institutions, creation of Urdu Department, provision of Urdu translators in government offices and so on) in which Muslims have higher stakes.

How deep is the exclusion of Muslims in the structures of wider opportunities? Of late, the Sachar Committee Report (2006) as well as empirically grounded research has brought to the fore under-representation of Muslims in socio-economic and other opportunities. Let us here take up some crucial parameters to gauge the extent of exclusion facing the Muslim community.

It is well known that education is a necessary precursor to socio-economic mobility. As a matter of fact, the positive outcomes of education are so huge and so crucial for human development that one often takes education as a single measure to assess the overall well-being of a population or a sub-set of it. Nationally, the Muslim community of India as a whole seems to cut a sorry figure in terms of literacy and education. The Sachar Committee Report sums up educational status of Muslims as thus:

> With regard to school education, the condition of Muslims is one of grave concerns. The data clearly indicates that while the overall levels of education in India measured through various indicators is still below universally acceptable standards, the educational status of the Muslim community in particular is a matter of great concern.......... When alternative indicators of educational achievement, more representative of the progress made in education, are considered, a significant disparity between the status of Muslims and that of other SRCs (except SCs/STs) can be noted. For example, both the Mean Years of Schooling and attendance levels of Muslims are low in absolute terms and in contrast to all SRCs except in some cases SCs/STs. In fact, in several contexts, SCs/STs are found to have overtaken Muslims.[7]

As also evident in Table 1, the literacy rate, one's ability to read, write and understand a simple statement, is lower among Muslims than among Hindus as a whole. Muslim children are less likely to attend schools and those attending are less likely to

7. Sachar Committee Report, 2006, chapter IV, p. 84

stay in schools for a few years. Muslims fall far behind Hindus in terms of completed levels of education. It has also been shown that they are far less likely to enter higher levels of education as compared to other religious groups (Hasan and Mehta, 2006; SCR, 2006).

Table 1: Literacy and Education among Muslims

Educational Indicators	Ref. Year	Hindus			Muslims
		General	OBC	SC/ST	
Literates (%)	2004–05	80.5	63.4	52.7	59.9
Proportion of children (6–14) attending school	2004–05	94.9	86.0	79.7	81.8
Graduates*	2004–05	15.3	4.4	2.2	3.4

Note: * for population age 20 years and above
Source: Sachar Committee Report, 2006

As in education, Indian Muslims also appear to be lagging behind other religious communities in the economic sphere. Prevalence of poverty is much higher among Muslims as compared to Hindus. Over one-third of Muslims live below the poverty line as against one-fourth among Hindus. Muslims living in urban areas are more likely to be poor than others, as well as their counterparts in rural areas (Shariff 1999, John and Mutatkar, 2005; SCR, 2006). Muslims have lower levels of consumption and lower levels of income compared to Hindus (Table 2) and disparities in consumption between Hindus and Muslims are even wider in urban areas.

Labour force participation rates of Muslims are also much lower than among other religious communities. For every hundred main workers among Hindus, there were 86 main workers among Muslims (Table 2). While the proportion of main workers among Muslims is lower, that of non-workers is higher. This indicates a higher unemployment rate among Muslims, though further questions need to be asked about the extent of the informal economic sector in relation to Muslims. Statistics indicate that the vast majority of workers among Muslims are concentrated in lower rungs of economic opportunities (Khalidi, 2006). Their participation in high earning jobs is low, too. The proportion of regular salaried persons of any social group is an indicator of income as well as material well-being. The representation of Muslims in this particular job category is much lower than among Hindus. For every hundred regular salaried workers among Hindus employed in the public sector, there were only 67 Muslims. The situation is even worse in the private sector, as Table 2 indicates.

Table 2: Economic Status of Muslims

Parameters	Ref. Year	All	Hindu	Muslim	Muslim/ Hindu Ratio
% Workers	2001				
Main workers		48.1	49.1	42.2	.86
Marginal workers		13.0	13.5	10.4	.77
Non-workers		38.9	37.5	47.5	1.27
% Regular salaried	2004–05				
Government sector		34.2	35.3	23.7	.67
Public/Private Ltd.		13.1	13.9	6.5	.47
Monthly per capita expenditure (current prices)	2004–05				
MPCE (Urban)		1105	1139	804	.70
MPCE (Rural)		579	568	553	.97
Incidence of poverty	2004–05				
Poverty ratio (Urban)		29	27	44	1.63
Poverty ratio (Rural)		28	28	33	1.78

Sources: Sachar Committee Report (2006).

In brief, if the above statistics reveal anything; they portray Muslims in disadvantaged positions in relation to Hindus at national level in India. Their overall access to available socio-economic opportunities is much less compared to Hindus as well as other religious communities. The stratum of lower socio-economic conditions is disproportionately large among Muslims.

The most disturbing fact is that while there has been substantial progress in the sum total of the socio-economic conditions of people in the country, the socio-economic conditions of Muslims have worsened during the last decade (Shariff and Razzack, 2006). As Reddy (2002) puts it:

"Whichever group of indicators one looks at and whatever level of detail of comparison, the story is the same. The Muslims are on the average on lower rungs of the socio-economic ladder than the Hindus and the differences either remained the same or widened during the 1990s."

If enhanced participation of the minorities forms the bedrock of national integration, it is the responsibility of the state to remove the hurdles that hinder their effective participation in the activities and opportunities enjoyed by the wider society. However, any attempt that privileges minority groups is bound to face tensions and resentment.

POLICY TENSIONS

Given that India has the world's most comprehensive affirmative action policy for addressing socio-economic advantages of backward communities,[8] glaring developmental deficits among Muslims have ignited intense debate on some kinds of affirmative action for them (Alam 2010). Nevertheless, there remains considerable confusion over the policy framework of affirmative action for addressing socio-economic exclusion facing the Muslims. The difficulties embedded in the formulation of and putting in place an affirmative action policy for Muslims are as follows.

---

8. In India, 'fixed quota' or 'reservation' of seats for the disadvantaged groups in legislatures, educational institutions and public employment is the dominant element of affirmative action policy. While the Scheduled Castes and Scheduled Tribes get benefits of reservation in legislatures, educational institutions and public employment, the OBCs are granted benefits of reservation in educational institutions and public employment only.

(a) ***Form (uniform vs. differentiated policy framework)***: The nature and severity of socio-economic disadvantages vary across social group. For instance, the disadvantages faced by the SCs/STs are not same as by the OBCs (other backward classes) and Muslims. The question that arises here is: whether a uniform or a differentiated policy framework should be adopted to address the disadvantages facing the Muslim community. To put it another way, whether the existing 'reservation' policy should be extended to cover the disadvantaged Muslim minorities or an alternative policy would better serve the purpose. If the policy of reservation is extended to Muslims, it will pacify the community elites. With this, the overall system will also acquire greater legitimacy. But given the socio-political climate in the country, such policy move would cause massive communal polarization. In case, an alternative policy framework (non-reservation) is designed for Muslims, such policy would be seen by Muslims as discriminatory, for it divides the 'disadvantaged' into 'deserving' and 'undeserving' based on religious affiliation.

(b) ***Selection of the beneficiary (individual vs. group)***: In Indian social context, no socio-cultural group, big or small, are internally homogeneous. They are hierarchically structured along multiple overlapping and intersecting socio-spatial networks of power. And the Muslim community is no exception (Ahmad 1978). Given this, individual rather than group may be preferred as the basis for selection of the beneficiaries. However, it may be argued that the Muslim community as a whole has been the victim of prejudices and discrimination due largely to historically embedded trajectories of communal relations and contestation for power. Hence, there is a justification for selecting whole group for the benefits of affirmative action policy. But if the avowed purpose of an affirmative action policy is rather helping out those at the bottom-of-the pyramid than social and political integration of the community/group elites, group based affirmative action policy is certainly a bad model. Research has shown that in a group based model of affirmative action, it is largely the well off section of the disadvantaged group that actually appropriates the benefits of the policy.

(c) ***Selection of areas/sectors (universalism vs. selectivism)***: This problem informs two policy dilemmas. One, Muslims are not evenly distributed across the states. A large portion of their population is concentrated in certain states and within state in certain districts. Moreover, the levels of their socio-economic backwardness vary a great deal across states and districts. So one may argue that let those geographical areas be identified for implementing affirmative action policy (in whatever form) which bear higher concentration of Muslims and are also deprived of socio-economic opportunities. While this approach might escape the allegation of 'minority appeasement', it is unlikely to pacify those who advocate for similar policy for addressing socio-economic backwardness of Muslims as for other backward communities.

The second dilemma is identification of sectors, that is, whether all sectors or only crucial sectors should be covered under affirmative action policy. This dilemma arises out of the nature of opposition to affirmative action policy in general. In India, although there is resentment and anger against affirmative action policy for the disadvantaged sections, its degree varies a great deal across sectors. Even reservation in educational institutions is generally much less controversial and contentious than in employment. Given the problem of communal backlash in the event of preferential treatment to Muslims in public employment, it can be suggested that affirmative action policy may begin with education and later on may be extended to other sectors (such as public employment) depending on how the policy is perceived by the majority community. Nonetheless, this approach faces the same problem as does the geographical approach.

(d) ***Net outcome (Consequentialism vs. welfarism; Cost vs. benefit)***: Any social policy has to be weighed against the net outcome it is likely to produce. The ratio of consequence (negative) to well being (in economic terms the ratio of cost to benefit) has to be assessed properly. Going by policy pragmatism, if the policy in question involves cost disproportionately higher than the benefit, it is better not to pursue. As past experience shows, affirmative action policy is a very sensitive issue both politically and socially. Affirmative action policy for religious minorities, Muslims in particular, is likely to generate huge communal backlash, which would cause more loss to them than benefits. If affirmative action policy for the Muslims is inevitable or unavoidable in the current circumstances, devising an affirmative action policy with minimal intended or unintended cost is a great social policy challenge facing the country.

The Upshot

The integration of minorities into national mainstream does not take place in vacuum. The process of integration is generally smooth where the minority groups are able to effectively participate in the opportunities available to the wider society. Thus, if national integration may be conceived as enhanced participation of ethnic or religious minorities, individually and as a group, in the wider socio-economic structures while having enough possibilities to retain the distinctive aspects of their culture and identity, there is an urgent need of re-orienting the prevailing discourse on national integration with reference to minority groups.

There are, of course, many issues relating to religio-cultural identity on which Muslims appeared to react/respond without having due respect to wider implications of their response for them as well as the nation at large. But actual behaviour of the Muslims or for that any deprived group needs to be understood in the context of severe deprivation and exclusion rather than within the framework of religio-cultural essentialism. For, identities based on religion, region and culture are dynamic and do not exist independent of wider structures and processes. They change with changing intellectual and material conditions of the groups and society at large. Therefore, the religio-cultural issues that may hinder integration of the minority groups cannot be addressed without looking at the larger issues of exclusion.

Persistent exclusion of minority groups has a long term deleterious impact on national integration. Gradually, it develops a sense of alienation among them, which eventually boils down to such activities that are inimical to national integration. Moreover, if a large minority group stands excluded, it can effectively impede socio-economic progress of the country. Either way, the process of national development and integration gets adversely affected.

Given the importance of enhanced participation of the minority groups in national development, the state is under obligation to frame appropriate 'inclusive' policies. However, the policies aimed at helping out the minority groups are not easy to formulate and implement. Such policies across the world generate considerable tensions. Given the fact that affirmative action policies generate tension and yet such policies are inevitable for larger national interests, the only way forward is mature engagement of the state, larger society and minority groups in question. As far as affirmative action policy for Muslims are concerned, the wider society has to acknowledge exclusion of Muslims and their impact on the process of national development. It should, therefore, help build up positive environment for instituting a long term and effective policy for social and economic uplift of the Muslims. The Muslims, on the other hand, should actively respond to the processes of socio-economic development rather than being passive recipients of the benefits doled out to them by the state. Only then they will become equal partners in contributing to and shaping the processes of national development.

REFERENCES

Ahmad, A. (1999): *Social Geography*. Jaipur: Rawat Publications.

Ahmad, Imtiaz (ed) (1978): *Caste and Social Stratification among Muslims* (New Delhi: Manohar, 1978).

Ahmad, S.N. (2004): *Origins of Muslim Consciousness in India*. London: Greenwood Press.

Alam, M. Sanjeer (2010): "Social Exclusion of Muslims in India and Deficient Debates About Affirmative Action: Suggestion for a New Approach, *South Asia Research*, Vol. 30 (1), pp. 43–65.

Drake, C. (1989): *National Integration in Indonesia* (Honolulu: University of Hawaii Press).

Dutt, A.K. and S. Devgun (1979): "Religious Pattern of India with a Factor Regionalization" *Geojournal*, Vol. 3 (2), pp. 201–13.

Gani, H.A. (1978): Muslim Political Issues and National Integration, New Delhi: Sterling Publishers.

Gopal Krishna (1977): Contemporary Muslim Attitudes and Their Place in Indian Society, (Mimeo), Delhi: CSDS.

Hasan, Mushirul (1997): *The Legacy of a Dived Nation*, New Delhi: Oxford University Press.

Hasan, Rana and A. Mehta (2006): 'Under-Representation of Disadvantaged Classes in Colleges: What Do the Data Tell Us?', *Economic and Political Weekly*, 41(35) (2 September): 3791–6.

Husain, S.A. (1965): *The Destiny of Indian Muslims* (New Delhi: Asia Publishing House.

Imam, Zafar (1978): "Some Aspects of the Social Structure" in Zafar Imam (ed.), *Muslims in India* New Delhi: Orient Longman, pp. 70–110.

John, Rijo M. and Rohit Mutatkar (2005): 'Statewise Estimates of Poverty Among Religious Groups in India', *Economic and Political Weekly*, 40(13) (26 March): 1337–45.

Khalidi, Omar (2006): *Muslims in Indian Economy*. Gurgaon: Three Essays Collective.

Lamb, B.P. (1968): *India: A World in Transition*, New York: Praeger Publishers.

Metcalf, Thomas. R (1997): *The Ideologies of Raj*, Cambridge: Cambridge University Press.

Miller, R.E. (1976): *Mappila Muslims of Kerala*, New Delhi: Orient Longman.

Murphy, G. (1953): *In the Minds of Men: The Study of Human Behaviour and Social Tension in India*, New York, p. 124.

Puri, Balraj (1993): "Indian Muslims since Partition" *Economic and Political Weekly*, Vol. 28 (40), pp. 2141–49.

Reddy, C. Rammanohar (2002): 'Deprivation Affects Muslims More', *The Hindu*, 12 September: 11.

Qureshi, I.H. (1956): *Muslims of Indo-Pak Subcontinent*, New Delhi: Renaissance Publication.

Sachar, Rajindar (2006): *Social, Economic and Educational Status of the Muslim Community of India. A Report*. New Delhi: Prime Minister's High Level Committee. Cabinet Secretariat. Government of India.

Seal, Anil (1968): *The Emergence of Indian Nationalism: Competition and Collaboration in the Late Nineteenth Century*. Cambridge: Cambridge University Press.

Shariff, Abusaleh and Azra Razzack (2006): '*Communal Relations and Social Integration* in *India: Social Development Report*. New Delhi: Oxford University Press.

Siddiqui, N.A. (1976): Population Geography of Muslims of India, New Delhi: S. Chand & C.O.

Sopher, D. (1956): "India's Language and Religion" *Focus*, Vol. 4 (6), pp. 1–6.

2
National Integration in India

*Mirza Asmer Beg**

National integration is an all-India exercise which can never be coercive but has to be based on consent. However, such a process, and its course, is wholly dependent upon a consensus on the understanding of this idea. But in India, we have found the term 'integration' to be quite bitterly contested, at the operational level. It has been construed by some to mean assimilation. Although in common usage, these two terms are often used interchangeably, but at a technical level, and especially in this context, both have very different connotations. According to the Oxford Dictionary, assimilation means 'absorb and incorporate', while integration means 'combining (one thing) with another to form a whole'. Moreover, in case of assimilation only one of the polity's nations will be privileged in the state-building effort, while the other "nations" would go unrecognized and may even be marginalized. (Alfred Stepan, Juan J. Linz and Yogendra Yadav: 2010) Nevertheless, if seen in its proper context and against the historical backdrop of its evolution, national integration is antithetical to assimilation.

MAJOR CHALLENGES

Since Indian unity is often conceived in terms of conformity or divergence to the great tradition, with its centrality of culture and religion, the integrational crisis continues to operate on the attitudinal level. Its interpretation in the pre-independence era in political idiom, led to Muslim separatism culminating in the

* Professor, Department of Political Science, AMU, Aligarh.

formation of Pakistan. It continues to alienate Minorities even now. The phenomena of Muslim, Tamil and tribal separatisms are basically reactions to a cultural proposition of Indian unity. It was this divergence which restricted the penetration of nationalist ideology among many sections of the Indian polity. In many cases, it forced them to reinforce their sub-national bias by patronizing an alien tradition, or by contemptuous negation of it. It restricted political participation and diffused the nationalistic urge into caste, communal or sectarian channels. (Kousar J. Azam: 1981)

The enterprise of national integration in India, therefore, faced these challenges. Over the years, we have seen in India that regional chauvinism and ultra-nationalism based on religious fundamentalism, threaten to submerge the different pluralities here. It also internally incites a chain of sub-nationalisms representing various suppressed or dormant nationalities and ethnicities. It appears now that those who thought of creating a modern nation state in India, had an insufficient understanding of the contradictions that were inherent in such an endeavour. Particularly, in view of the fact that the nation was required to be built on a social ground that was full of not just numerous diversities but also of gross disparities which was not to be reduced by the new structure of a state, but be accentuated, rather frozen by it. As the country moves towards the 21st century, it is going to face this shift from integrative to disintegrative tendencies more sharply than was the case during a large part of the 20th century. Today we look at the diverse types of attrition that the nation-state in India finds itself facing.

Slowly and incrementally we have been seeing a gradual wearing down of the legitimacy of the state for the people of India, both in respect of its standing for those who for long depended on it for their well-being and in respect of its credibility in the eyes of the middle class professionals. Moreover, there has taken place, over the years, a gradual erosion of authority, *vis-a-vis* the appearance and splendor with which the state was looked up to, both by the citizens at large and, in respect of the authority of the centre, by intermediate and local units, institutions of the state and other institutions of civil society. The mounting challenges to state authority by a whole range of regional movements have rendered the state an arena of ever-increasing conflicts and violence. And also there has taken place an erosion of the whole notion of the uniqueness and supremacy of the Indian state both in relation to other centers of power within the country and as regards external interests, which has led to a declining emphasis on things like autonomy and freedom. The state's capability to facilitate national integration has consequently got debilitated.

To add to the sorry state of affairs, we have concerns like poverty and poor healthcare, which are no less disintegrative. India is still a very poor country with around 44 per cent of the population earning lass than a dollar a day. The poorest 20 per cent of the Indians have more than twice the rate of mortality, malnutrition and fertility compared to the richest 20 per cent. However, India has one of the most privatized healthcare systems in the world and less than a fifth of all the healthcare coming from the government. In U.K. the share of government spending is over 90 per cent and in the US 44 per cent. (Usha Rai: 2005). It really comes as a shock to find that healthcare here is more privatized than even the U.S. which is the *Mecca* of privatization.

Over the years, minorities, especially Muslims in India, have learnt to live as children of a lesser God, in life-long fear of attack because of their religious identity; of profiling as terrorists or criminals; of facing daily discrimination and distrust when they look for a house or employment: their ghettoes denied public services like drinking water and education. (Harsh Mander: 2011). The state in India has tried to walk a tight rope between the requirement of religious liberty that frequently entails non-interference in the affairs of religious communities, and the demand for equality and justice which necessitates intervention in religiously sanctioned social customs. (T.N. Srinivasan: 2006). The liberal Indian democratic state in the name of minority cultural rights, grants to minorities (in the Indian case, to Muslims) their own special personal laws on divorce, marriage, alimony, etc., even if some of these laws are parochial in various respects. On this reading, the state may grant to the minority Muslim community their own *alternative nomic or customary system*, which is a rival system to liberal law, with its own sort of right or truth on its side, and the pluralism that the constitution was committed to must acknowledge this fact. (Akeel Bilgrami: 2011) The state, however, has not yet been able to resolve this conundrum.

Muslims have also been seen to be under-represented in Legislative bodies. The primary reason for Muslim under-representation is their under-nomination by political parties. In the first-past-the-post system, parties tend to favour the majority community. Under the growing influence of Hindutva, many parties have also been reluctant to nominate Muslims, although they might be strong candidates. If Muslim "deprivation" or under-representation in the Lok Sabha is measured in relation to their population, it is pretty pervasive nationally (47 per cent). It is particularly high in Rajasthan (91 per cent), Gujarat (82 per cent), Delhi (86 per cent), Maharashtra (71 per cent), Madhya Pradesh (50 per cent), and Tamil Nadu (53 per cent). Even in Kerala and West Bengal, with a strong Muslim presence, the deprivation rate exceeds 40 per cent.

When the Constituent Assembly debated and rejected reservation of legislative seats for the religious minorities in 1949, Nehru called it "an act of faith above all for the majority community because they will have to show after this that they can behave to others in a generous, fair and just way [by keeping their representation commensurate with their population]. Let us live up to that faith." India has not lived up. (Nazeeruddin: 2012)

For effective participation of minorities in the politics of the country, we might need adoption of an electoral system of Proportional Representation (PR) with waiver of the requirement of minimum electoral support ('threshold clause') for minorities. Where PR is not in operation we could have: (*i*) avoidance of gerrymandering in constituency formation, as there are evidences to support this contention that the exercise of delimitation often works to the disadvantage of the Muslims, and (*ii*) adequate number of special, additional designated constituencies reserved for minority electorate. Further, attention needs to be paid to the recruitment of minorities into positions in central administration (particularly army, police, judiciary and intelligence services).

The concern for provision of mechanisms for effective participation of minorities derives from the experience that even the limited rights of minorities to enjoy their own culture, to profess and practice their own religion and to use their own language guaranteed in Article 27 of the International Covenant On Civil and Political Rights (ICCPR) cannot be realized without their effective participation in the political process as enunciated in Article 2.2, 2.3 and 2.4 of the UN Declaration on the Rights of Persons Belonging to National or Ethnic, Religions and Linguistic Minorities. (Iqbal A. Ansari: 2001)

Since independence, the aggressive tendencies of dominant linguistic groups to impose their language on others, has led to much violence and conflict. Absence of a suitable scheme of language has slowly led to greater disaffection. Deceitful mishandling of the language problem had provided a key plank for political mobilization to political parties. Regionalism has, consequently obstructed the process of integration. And then there is the ferment of zones of conflict, in the nation's north-western and north-eastern peripheries, as much as in the central forested heartlands. Here people have taken up arms against the state, for diverse claims of self-determination, ethnic assertion and a more egalitarian society.

Moreover, the most disintegrative process which has been unleashed in India and which is slowly cutting at the roots of our nation is the economic policies which have been in effect for the last twenty odd years. Disparities in incomes are rising by the day. In the last six years since 2005–06, the Government of India wrote off corporate income tax worth Rs. 3,74,937 crore, in successive Union budgets. In the last budget it was Rs. 88,263 crore, compared to this, the Rs. 1.54 crore in subsidy to poor and farmers, seems like peanuts. In fact, the daily average net per capita availability of food-grains for the last five years is actually lower than it was in 1955–59. Despite this, instead of helping the poor, the national health budget was progressively reduced to 0.9 per cent of the GDP in the 90s. It remains to be raised, despite all promises to do so by the Government.

Now, the Government wants to have FDI in retail, thereby, opening up a sector that for all its warts presently employs about 44 million people and has total sales of close to $400 billion. It wants to do this after a decade of other counter-effective policies, which were apparently intended at 'benefitting' the farmers. The consequence was a big increase in the indebtedness of the peasantry and the worst-ever wave of farmer suicides. Moreover, we have seen seven and a half million people abandon agriculture in a decade. Now, the same people are promising the moon for the farmers. It appears too good to be true. (Mirza Asmer Beg: 2012)

As a consequence today a large number of our fellow citizens live below the poverty line. About 800 million Indians survive at less than Rs. 20 a day. Their condition seems more inhuman, if we look at the 100 thousand dollar millionaires that India has. We have four Indians in the list of the ten richest people in the world. On the other hand, India figures at number 67 in the Global Hunger Index. India is estimated to add more hungry people to the global population of hungry people in the next five years, than the whole world combined. Lakhs of farmers have committed suicides in the last several years, due to unbearable economic problems. (Mirza Asmer Beg: 2012) All these factors provide an ideal breeding ground for naxalism, terrorism and crime. They threaten and question the very existence and legitimacy of the state. We need to remind ourselves that it is the loss of hope among sections of frustrated youth in the law-enforcement and justice system, which provides a fertile ground for such divisive tendencies. Given such circumstances, integration or coming together appears to be a distant dream.

In addition, the problem of casteism breeds 'internal exclusions' (Bhargava: 2004) within a religious group. It leads to injustice, exclusion and bigotry within a religious community, and it, therefore, results in the perpetuation of intra-religious disintegrative tendencies. The oppressed sections are repeatedly made conscious of their 'inferior' social identity and are not allowed to integrate and participate in the larger national enterprise of development.

Another major issue is corruption, which becomes an issue of concern because of its far-reaching and lasting negative consequences. It is anti-poor and anti-national. It almost always advantages the powerful and rich and discriminates against the weak and poor. Although corruption is a global phenomenon, we have seen countries which were highly corrupt till very recently, reforming themselves and getting the benefits of good governance in a short time. A case in point is Singapore.

THE FUTURE

In India, the main problem with us is not that we have different identities, but that they are wrongly prioritized. Our national identity is suppressed under other parochial and narrow identities. The political discourse in India, ably assisted by the media, tries to reinforce these identities, at the cost of national identity. The need of the hour is for all of us, and especially the media to understand this serious problem. The responsibility of the media becomes greater because of its vast reach. It plays one of the most prominent roles in the socialization of the masses. If today, the media here becomes more conscious of its responsibility, instead of being conscious of its power, to be able to show and explain things, without seeing them in broad 'national context', it would be doing a great service to the cause of national integration in India.

The media's contribution towards integrating India could be more useful and productive, if people here become more discerning and slowly stop patronizing the kind of stuff being fed to us by the media, which is totally insensitive to the 'national concerns'. It is a two-way road, where the masses and the media both have to play a role. (Mirza Asmer Beg: 2010)

We need to address long-standing conflict zones with a new human approach. Reconciliation and forgiveness are required, but we must also see remorse and apology. The guilty must be brought to book, as peace and unity can only come when there is justice. Forgetting pogroms like Nellie in Assam (1983) and Gujarat (2002) is not the solution. Because if we settle for the past as some would like it scripted, we threaten the meaning of our present, and endanger our future. These contestations are not just about many battles in courtrooms that must be waged. The contestation is about the meaning of citizenship. It is about the relationship between citizen and State. It is about challenging State impunity. *It* is the battle for collective memory against forgetting because it is ultimately the battle for the idea of India. (Farah Naqvi: 2012) Without justice, we cannot move on. Hence, we need to stoutly pursue justice in cases of gross human rights violations. For example in Kashmir, investigators working for the State Human Rights Commission have reported that 2730 unidentified people alleged to be terrorists lie buried in makeshift graveyards across the State. The debate on this issue now threatens to turn into an unproductive polemical exchange between human rights groups and the government. But this exercise is meaningless for those who lost their loved ones. There are concrete things that need to be done to give these families a sense of closure and justice. DNA samples could be taken from the bodies of the dead and matched against results from the families of missing persons. Forensic pathologists could examine the bodies where there is reason to suspect extrajudicial execution. (Hindu: 2011.) The policy of indefinite deferral does no good, if the hearts and minds of the people have to be knit together.

There is a need for the political class, the civil society groups and public intellectuals to get the conceptual scheme of national integration redefined in human rights perspective. The pre-independence discourse under secular-communal paradigm requires a shift towards new norms of inclusiveness and multiculturalism, which happily got occasionally reflected in statements and resolutions of the Indian National Congress during the freedom struggle. Under the international human rights standards, inclusive democratic integration means providing genuine equality to underrepresented minorities, both religious and linguistic, by special measures, so that all national institutions in the common public sphere become socially diverse with effective representation of minorities. It is by sharing the public space in schools-colleges, the work place, the residential areas and decision making forums and legislatures that communities get integrated. In this regard we have still a long way to go. There are not one but many battles yet to be waged, and numerous more to be won.

We also need to realize that coercion in achieving uniformity would be counter-productive. For example, in matters of civil laws, some in India argue that for national integration to actualize, we need to enforce a uniform civil code in the country. But unfortunately, that is not the solution. The time has come now to accept the human rights norm of multiculturalism, requiring pluralism of family laws, provided no community based law is in contravention of human rights of any of its members, i.e., women or children.

However, there are beacons of light in this darkness. In the political arena, political parties are slowly realizing that emotive issues have a short shelf-life and they have no option but to turn to real issues if they have to survive in politics. It is now becoming politically profitable to build primary schools, roads and healthcare centers. This maturity would help us come out of the vicious circle of political parties selling pseudo-issues and people rushing towards them because of the emotive sugar coating on their respective vested interests. Earlier, political parties were generally not required to perform *vis-s-vis* real issues as they were inconsequential issues in the electoral arena. Things now appear to be changing. The developments in Bihar and some other states are indicative of a new brand of politics, based on real issues.

In the civil society also there appears to be a growing realization that the future of India does not lie in exclusivism. The recent history of world politics has shown that societies which have thrived and prospered are the ones which are based on inclusivisim and tolerance. Fortunately, these notions have historically been the underlying basis of the 'idea of India'. The impediments are many, but we all need to try to actualize this 'idea'. Only this can guarantee a safe, secure and prosperous future for all of us.

REFERENCES

1. Ansari, Iqbal. A. (2001): Ensuring representation, *Seminar*. No. 506, October.
2. Azam, Kousar J. (1981): *Political Aspects of National Integration*. Meenakshi Publications. Delhi. p. 35.
3. Beg, Mirza Asmer, (2010): National Integration: The Indian Experience, in A.R. Kidwai (ed.) Higher Education: Issues and Challenges. pp. 22–27.

4. Beg, Mirza Asmer (2012): Economic Democracy: The Need of the Hour. Editorial in *Lokniti Newsletter*. January.

5. Rajeev Bhargava (2004): Inclusion and exclusion in South Asia: The Role of Religion, OCCASIONAL PAPER, Background paper for HDR 2004, United Nations Development Programme.

6. Bilgrami, Akeel (2011): *Secularism: Its Content and Context*. October. SSRC Working Papers. Columbia University.

7. Editorial (2011): *The Hindu*, 30 September.

8. Mander, Harsh (2011): A fractured freedom, *The Hindu Magazine*, August 14.

9. Nazeeruddin (2012): Muslim Minority Exclusion and Development Issues: Need for Inclusive Policy. *Zenith: International Journal of Multidisciplinary Research*. Vol. 2 Issue 1, January.

10. Naqvi, Farah (2012): The Battle Against Forgetting. *The induHiHindu*, February, 28.

11. Rai, Usha, (2005): Medicare: Majority remains in poor health. *The Tribune*. Chandigarh, Sept. 24.

12. Srinivasan, T.N. (ed.) (2006): The Distinctiveness of Indian Secularism. *The Future of Secularism*, Oxford University Press, Delhi, pp. 20–53.

13. Stepan, Alfred, Juan J. Linz and Yogendra Yadav (2010): The Rise of 'State-Nations'. *Journal of Democracy*. Volume 21 (3), July. pp. 50–68.

3

Multilingualism and National Integration

S. Imtiaz Hasnain

INTRODUCTION

Calamity, despite causing social, psychological and emotional discomfiture, dispossession and dislocation at an individual, societal or national level also provides a sure test of gauging the sanity of individuals in society. In a state of calamity, a sense of emotional oneness and shared sentiments of belongingness assume significance for preserving the oneness of nation and nationality – India as a nation and Indian as one's nationality, irrespective of differences on account of race, religion, language and script. History is replete with such instances. Perhaps one may revoke, as a reminder, the incarnation or emergence of Mrs. Indira Gandhi as 'Durga' during the period that preceded and followed the formation of Bangladesh. What clearly emerges from this state of crises or calamity is the integration of an individual and society with the welfare and protection of the nation as a whole.

But the crises are not always there to stay. India as a nation state has several kinds of diversity – language being one of them, and therefore it becomes imperative on the part of the government to involve certain strategies for bringing together national integration, which can allow the celebration of linguistic diversity and let the people live together separately. The Constitution of India provides adequate safeguards for preserving linguistic and cultural identities. Before we discuss the necessary provisions that the nation as a whole takes upon itself to forge national integration in relation to language, the following sections will highlight the multiplicity of race, religion, language and script in India and Indian multilingualism. The subsequent sections will discuss the constitutional provisions related to language matters and the steps taken in the interest of national integration as reflected through the language policy of India.

MULTIPLICITY OF RACE, RELIGION, LANGUAGE AND SCRIPT

India is a country with a multiplicity of race, religious groups, language and script. Many different human races have been living together for thousands of years, which include the Australoids and Veddids from Srilanka, Negritoids from the Andaman Islands, dark Melano-Indians, fair North Indians and yellow Mongoloids.

India presents a highly diversified religious panorama with five important religions of native origin – Hinduism, Jainism, Buddhism and Sikhism. Besides, there are numerous tribal religions and four non-Indian faiths, namely, Islam, Christianity, Judaism and Mazdaism.

If one looks at the linguistic map of India, one finds bewildering variety of languages represented by five language families, namely Indo-Aryan, Dravidian, Austro-Asiatic, Tibeto-Burman and Andamanese. Recent research finding indicates the possibilities of establishing a sixth language family of India called Great Andamanese, which is an isolate and distinctly different from Andamanese. India as a home to so many languages has also been a space, which can be characterized as multi-centric space. Though it may seem contradictory, nevertheless it is true that India is one nation and many at the same time, one culture and many. It is, therefore, no wonder that its linguistic boundaries are not rigidly fixable, and the pressure of living together for thousands of years has served to create 'India as a linguistic area'.

This concept was first given by Emeneau in 1958, which subsequently found support from research findings of other scholars. It may also be mentioned here that this idea had been latent in the research findings of Suniti Kumar Chatterjee way back in 1926. The multiplicity of linguistic scene that was obtained in India has been recorded in Census documents, and the monumental survey conducted by Sir George Abraham Grierson (1851–1941), an Irish philologist who joined the Indian Civil Service in 1873. He was designated superintendent of the newly sanctioned *Linguistic Survey of India* in 1898.

Quite unlike the modern Indian languages that belong to different language families, modern Indian scripts have originated from a single script called the *Brahmi* script. The earliest recorded evidence of the Brahmi script can be found in Ashokan inscriptions of the third century B.C. Although this script was in use in the rest of the country, in North-West India and Central Asia there existed a parallel script called *Kharosthi* from the time of Ashoka until about the fourth century A.D. Diversification of the *Brahmi* script continued and towards the close of the ancient period of Indian history it developed into two subtypes conventionally known as Northern and Southern types. The Northern type led to the rise of the Gupta script of the fourth and fifth centuries A.D. Subsequently it became the basis for the emergence of an amazing range of different subtypes known as *Sharda* script and its variants like *Landa* script, *Gurumukhi* script, *Takri* script, and *Kutila* (bent) script and its variants like *Nagari* script, *Kaithi* script, *Modi* script and proto-probangali script etc. the Southern type of the *Brahmi* script gave rise to the Kannada-Telugu and Tamil-Malayalam scripts. In addition to the *Brahmi* script, the *Kufi* and *Naskh* scripts also came into existence at a later stage. The People of India (POI) project identified the total number of twenty five scripts of which there are eleven major scripts mostly employed by the speakers of the Scheduled Languages, thirteen minor scripts and Roman script. The multiplicity of scripts also finds its expression in the manner in which speakers switch from one script to another to mark the assertion of one's identity. For instance, the Roman script was introduced for the Konkani language (now a Scheduled Language) to stress its identity as different from that of Marathi, or use of the *Ol Chiki* script (introduced by Pandit Raghunath Murmur) along with Roman script used for Santali language as an effort to define and assert one's identity.

INDIAN MULTILINGUALISM

India has always been a multilingual country, and multilingualism is one of the most distinguishing features and an all-pervading element of the Indian society. As Chatterjee (1972) notes:

> *But for 3000 years and more, to say the least, there has beene interaction among the four great Speech-Families of India-the Indo-Aryan (Indo-European), Dravidian, Austric (Munda or Kol and Mon-Khmer) and Sino-Tibetan. As a result of this the corners of these languages groups so to say have been largely rubbed off, resulting in the evolution of a common pan-Indian Speech-Culture type which we have mainly inherited, and which has brought us together, whether we are superficially or deeply within the smaller circles of Indo-Aryan or Dravidian, Austric or Sino-Tibetan.*
>
> (cited in Hasnain, 2010:78)

This unique diversity oflanguages makes India a 'sociolinguistic giant' and a language laboratory for the study of dynamics of languages in contact and strategies of communication.

Indian multilingualism is not only a distinguishing feature of the Indian society but it is also unique in the sense that it enjoys the status of being both 'plurilingual' and 'multilingual'. Contrary to the common perception where the two terms are treated synonymously, both 'multilingual' and 'plurilingual' have hyponymous status involving the notion of inclusion. Inclusion is a matter of class membership in which 'multilingual' is the 'upper' term called superordinate and 'plurinlingual' is the lower term called hyponym. In plurilingual situation the main languages are recognized as official languages, while in multilingual situation the country may have many languages but for practical purposes only some are considered official. Although one may find clear-cut instances of plurilingualism in case of Singapore and Switzerland, one can still find logic of plurilingualism in Indian context as well in which the major languages of different states are considered for official purposes. For example, Tamil is used in Tamil Nadu, Telugu in Andhra Pradesh, Punjabi in Punjab, etc. Multilingual situation in India needs no elaboration as there are Scheduled Languages recognized by the Constitution of India and for practical purposes only some are exclusively considered official. Thus, out of 1576 classified mother tongues based on 1991 census, 234 are identifiable with returns of 10,000 plus speakers out of which there are twenty two Scheduled Languages (after 100th Amendment to the Constitution), twenty four languages given recognition by the Sahitya Akademi, thirty five languages used in newspapers and periodicals, sixty seven languages used for primary education, eighty languages used by National Literacy Mission for imparting literacy, and 104 languages used in AIR broadcasts.

In spite of linguistic diversity, multilingualism has not been a problem for communication. On the contrary it facilitates communication and has contributed to the cultural unity of the country, which finds its expression in the creation of link language (e.g. Hindustani) and pidgins. Pidgins bind mutually unintelligible disparate languages together, and in the Indian context we find *Sadari, Nagamese, Desia*, etc. as examples of pidgins. Indian multilingualism is a norm and accepted linguistic behaviour where different languages are constantly maintained by using them for performing different functions in different domains of activity but still keeping the structure distinct. In fact, the most relevant characteristic of Indian multilingualism, which makes it a natural state of language behavior, has been its 'allocation of social roles to different languages falling within the range of verbal repertoire of a given speech community. The non-competing nature of these roles sustained the non-conflicting and socially stable pattern (of multilingualism).' (Srivastava, 1980) Hence, in the Indian multilingualism context it is fairly common to find non-competing nature of allocation of social roles to different languages in one's language situation in which L1 may be used for intimate communication, L2 for proximate communication, L3 for professional and elite communication, L4 for entertainment, L5 for religious purpose and L6 for higher research.

LANGUAGE MATTERS AND CONSTITUTION OF INDIA: REFLECTION ON LANGUAGE POLICY

All language matters pertain to issues concerning official language of the Union and the States, use of Devanagari script, language of the Supreme Court, High Court, etc, Special Directives are dealt with under different Articles in Part XVII of the Constitution, while Part V and Part VI deal with the languages to be used in the Union and the States. The Constituent Assembly passed the Part XVII on 14th September 1949.

In Part XVII of the Constitution there are four Chapters dealing with language matters, which are covered under different Articles.

Chapter I: Language of the Union

It includes the following two Articles:

Article 343 recognizes Hindi in Devanagari script as the official language of the Union and "for a period of fifteen years from the commencement of the Constitution, the English language shall continue to be used for all the official purposes of the Union for which it was being used immediately before such commencement." However "... Parliament may by law provide for the use, after the said period of fifteen years … the English language … or such purposes may be specified in the law."

Article 344 enables the President to constitute an Official Language Commission after 5 years and then suggests reviewing the progress made by Hindi after 10 years.

Chapter II: Regional languages

It includes the following three Articles:

Article 345 empowers the Legislature of the State to adopt "any one or more languages in use in the State or Hindi as the language or languages to be used for all or any of the official purposes" of the concerned State.

Article 346 stipulates that the official language of the Union "shall be the official language for communication between one State and another State, and between a State and the Union." If two or more States agree that Hindi language shall be the official language for communication between such states, that language may be used for such communication.

Article 347 states that on demand being made "the President may, if he is satisfied that a substantial proportion of the population of a State desire the use of any language spoken by them to be recognized by that State" and may direct that such language shall also be recognized throughout that State or any part thereof.

Chapter III: Language of the Supreme Court, High Court, etc.

It includes the following two Articles;

Article 348 stipulates that English shall be the language of the Supreme Court and the High Courts until the Parliament by a law otherwise provides. Similarly, the authoritative texts of Acts, the language of Bills, bye-laws, rules, regulations, etc shall also be in English.

Article 348 (3) stipulates that in cases in which a State has prescribed any language other than English for use Bills or Acts passed by the Legislature "a translation of the same in the English language published under the authority of the Governor of the State in the Official Gazette of that shall be deemed to be the authoritative text."

Article 349 stipulates that no change in the language of Bills, bye-laws, Rules, Acts, Regulations, as mentioned in Article 348 (1), can be contemplated for 15 years and after that period the President must be satisfied about the need for a change.

Chapter IV: Special Directives

It includes the following two Articles;

Article 350 provides for "every person to submit a representation for the redress of any grievance to any officer or authority of the Union or a State in any of the languages used in the Union or the State, as the case may be."

Article 350 A stipulates that "It shall be the endeavour of every State and of every local authority within the State to provide adequate facilities for instruction in the mother tongue at the primary stage of education to children belonging to linguistic minority groups; and the President may issue such directions to any State as he considers necessary or proper for securing the provision of such facilities."

Articles 350 B stipulates that "There shall be a Special Officer for linguistic minorities to be appointed by the President. It shall be the duty of the Special Officer to investigate all matters relating to the safeguards provided for linguistic minorities under this Constitution and report to the President upon those matters at such intervals as the President may direct, and the President shall cause all such reports to be laid before each House of Parliament and sent to the governments of the States concerned."

Article 351 is devoted to the development of Hindi. It stipulates that " It shall be the duty of the Union to promote the spread of the Hindi language, to develop it so that it may serve as a medium of expression for the elements of the composite culture of India and to secure its enrichment by assimilating, without interfering with the genius, forms, style and expressions used in Hindustani and in the other languages of India specified in the Eighth Schedule, and by drawing, wherever necessary or desirable, for its vocabulary primarily on Sanskrit and secondarily on other languages."

In Part V and Part VI, the Articles 120 and 210, respectively, deal with the languages to be used in the Union and the States (not as the official language of the Union and the States, which is covered under Articles 343 and 345). Both the Articles (120 and 210) give power to the presiding offices of the Union and the State legislatives to use their discretion to allow any member to speak in his mother tongue if he is unable to speak in the recognized official language or languages. It further states that facilities to translate the speeches from mother tongues to official language(s) and *vice versa* shall, however, not be provided. It may be mentioned here that Articles 120 and 210 refer to the language (s) to be used only in the legislatures of the Union and the State, where as Articles 343 and 345 refer to the language (s) to be used in the Executive and Judiciary of the union and the States. Further, since these two Articles (343 and 345) stipulate Hindi and " one or more of the languages is use in the State or Hindi as the official language or languages of that State; the question of mother tongues does not arise here (Parts V and VI were passed on 12th September 1949)"

SENSITIVITY TO LANGUAGE OF MINORITY

Concern towards the sensitivity and welfare of the minority defines the civility of governance of a nation. In terms of language India is a country of linguistic minorities. If we look at the minority with reference to language, one finds the sensitivity addressed by the framers of our Constitution. Although precise definition of the term 'minority' has eluded the framers of Indian Constitution as well as the international instruments, Indian Constitution provides certain rights to the minorities to preserve their language, religion and culture, and even enjoins upon the government under special directives to use and safeguard the interest of minority languages in education and protect them from discrimination. In Article 29 the Constitution provides explicit guarantee for the protection of minorities:

Article 29 (1) stipulates that "Any section of the citizens residing in the territory of India or any part thereof having a distinct language, script or culture of its own shall have the right to conserve the same."

(2) "No citizen shall be denied admission into any educational institution maintained by the State or receiving aid out of State funds on grounds only of religion, race, caste, language or any of them."

Interest of minority languages in education and protection from discrimination can be seen in Article 30.

Article 30 (1) states that "All minorities, whether based on religion or language, shall have the right to establish and administer educational institutions of their choice."

(1a) "In making any law providing for the compulsory acquisition of any property of any educational institution established and administered by a minority, referred to in clause I, the State shall ensure that the amount fixed by or determined under such law for the acquisition of such property is such as would not restrict or abrogate the right guaranteed under that clause."

"The State shall not, in granting aid to educational institutions, discriminate against any educational institution on the ground that it is under the management of a minority, whether based on religion or language."

The second clause, in fact, enables linguistic minorities to claim state aid for running their educational institutions.

THE THREE LANGUAGE FORMULA

The three language formula is yet another step towards promoting national integration on account of diverse linguistic heterogeneity. The spirit behind this was that at least three languages, namely the mother tongue or the languages of the region where the child lives, Hindi as an official language of the country, and a modern European language, preferably English (in order to cope with the demands of science and technology) have to be learnt at the school level. The chief ministers of States and Central Ministry in the meeting held on August 10–12, 1961 approved the three-language formula. The simplified three language formula reads as follows:

(a) The regional language and mother tongue when the latter is different from the regional language;
(b) Hindi or in Hindi speaking areas, another Indian language; and
(c) English or any other modern European language

The National Policy on Education (NPE) subsequently came into existence, in 1986, which recommended the formula in the following ways:

(a) Hindi, English and a modern Indian language (preferably one of the Southern languages) in Hindi speaking areas, and
(b) The regional language, Hindi and English in non-Hindi speaking areas.

The letter and spirit of the three-language formula supported and encouraged national integration. But how far the implementation of this formula has succeded in achieving the desired objective of national integration remains to be seen.

LANGUAGE INSTITUTIONS

Setting up of various language institutions is helpful for funding and monitoring the language development and promotional activities and programmes taken up by various states. Thus, the following language institutions have been set up by the Govt. of India with the objective of developing Indian languages for use in Education:

(a) The Commission for Scientific and Technical Terminology (CSTT)
(b) Central Hindi Directorate (CHD)
(c) National Council for the Promotion of Urdu language (NCPUL)
(d) Central Institute of Hindi (CHI)
(e) Central Institute of Indian Languages (CIIL)
(f) National Council for the Promotion of Sindhi Language (NCPSL)
(f) National Council of Educational Research and Training (NCERT)
(h) State Council of Educational Research and Training (SCERT)

CONCLUSION

Language is a central feature for forming cultural identity. It also functions as a political symbol for integration of major groups. National integration presupposes new channel and network of communication and it is the language that binds the network. Decisions of language policy have strong bearing on the architecture of the nation. Language diversity and linguistic pride and heritage of the speaking community should be maintained and safeguarded for appreciating the values of alterity. The efforts to promote simultaneity of multilingualism and national integration will give best results only when the gap between constitutional provisions and social and political performance is bridged.

REFERENCES

Benedikter, Thomas (2009): *Language Policy and Linguistic Minorities in India: An appraisal of the linguistic rights of minorities in India*. New Brunswick and London: LIT Verlag Transaction Publishers.

Hasnain, S. Imtiaz (2001): Place of minority languages in education. In C.J. Daswani (ed.) *Language Education in Multilingual India*. UNESCO Publication.

Hasnain, S. Imtiaz (2010): Multilingualism. In A.R. Kidwai (ed.) *Higher Education: Issues and Challenges*. New Delhi, Mumbai, Chennai: Viva Books.

Koul, Omkar Nath (2009): National integration and multilingualism: India's reality show. In Shailendra Kumar Singh (ed.) *Rethinking Multilingualism: Issues and Problems*. Guwahati: EBH Publishers.

4

From Explicit Contradictions to Implicit Unity: The Trajectory of National Integration in India

K.C. Sreekumar

In this paper I make an attempt to answer five pertinent questions: first, why the question of national integration in India? second, how national integration should be brought about in a multicultural society? third, what are the major challenges to national unity that the country faced after independence? fourth, how did the political system face these challenges? and fifth, what lessons the future policy makers can learn from these?

I

The question of national integration assumes significance because most of the modern states are ethnically heterogeneous. National integration implies the fostering of nationalism among the people of a country. The classical concept about a nation-state is that of an ethnic group having their own independent politico-economic system. But this type of ethnic homogeneity was and still is very rare. Anthony Smith observes: "clearly, the very term 'nation-state is a misnomer. Ethnic pluralism rather than ethnic homogeneity appears still to be the norm, despite the acceptance of the principle of self-determination" (Smith. A 10). Most of the states in the world of today are composed of two or more ethnic communities. Both large and small states possess sizeable minorities and most states have small ethnic minorities. One observer had noted that out of one hundred and thirty two independent states in 1971, only twelve were ethnically homogeneous, representing 9.1 per cent of the total. Another twenty five (or 18.9 per cent) had a single ethnic community comprising over 90 per cent of the state's population. A further twenty five had a single ethnic community comprising 75–89 per cent of the population and thirty one states had an ethnic community representing 50–74 per cent of the state's population. On the other side, in thirty nine states (or 29.5 per cent), the largest ethnic group comprised less than 50 per cent of the population; while in fifty three states (40.2 per cent) the population was divided into more than five significant groups (Connor 320). Centuries of conquest and population movement resulted in the geographical intermingling of many cultural groups in a complex pattern. So the nationalist image of the world consisting of states based on culturally distinctive groups occupying homogeneous, compact and mutually exclusive national territories is far from reality. Sharing this view, Cornelia Navari writes, "If we ask when such a state of affairs came into being we should say, at no time." (13). Hugh Tinker also subscribes to this view (119). Breuilly also observes that the measurement of cultural homogeneity or heterogeneity is, in any case, at best highly uncertain (223).

In the opinion of Rupert Emerson former colonies in Asia and Africa would face grave threats to their national integrity because a large fraction of the peasantry never had any involvement in the national integration or organization (173–74). In the post-independence phase their pre-nationalist group loyalty gets re-asserted due to struggle for power between the competing domestic forces. According to a Soviet social scientist, inter-state and intra-state conflicts attained momentum in most of the Asian and African countries after independence (Sumoniya 6–16). But this situation changed after independence. Nationalism is no longer a reaction to outside interference. At this stage the process of social demarcation gains significance.

These facts emphasise the economic aspect of liberation struggle. With the attainment of independence the Afro-Asian countries entered into a new stage of prolonged struggle for socio-political stabilization and national consolidation. The economic development of these countries depends on the fulfillment of these tasks. But often political factors hamper economic development. The past experience is that, in many countries activities aimed at national integration and national-state construction caused an increase in tensions and conflicts between ethnic factors alone. Behind ethnic differences there were other important differences in the level of socio-economic and political development of the nation, nationalities and tribes concerned.

There are many reasons why this has not occurred so seriously before independence. The colonial ruler favoured no group in particular and hence the internal rivalries were left in a state of suspended animation. Moreover, the need to secure freedom helped the unification of all political forces within the country. But the dawn of self government effected a drastic change in this situation. Not only that. Before independence the different nationalities and tribes were in a state of isolation from one another. This isolation, the insignificance of inter-ethnic contacts, the possession of land on the basis of traditional law, traditional specialisation of profession etc. prevented the development of inter-ethnic contradictions. However, this situation under-went a change after independence. Members of all nationalities secured equal prescribed right to all forms of social and political activity. But this could not be practised due to socio-economic and cultural differences. As a result each group tries to have control over the state. Different social forces would try for a unified statehood, if they have a real chance of bringing it under their control (Iondansky).

In many of the former colonies the anti – colonial nationalist movement was built upon a series of lower level conflicts and identities rather than substituting their own new identities in place of the lower-level ones. This was necessitated by the heterogeneous nature of the population. Thus primordial loyalty lingers on even after independence. Conflict is inherent in such a society of diversity. But this does not mean that cultural homogeneity would prevent conflicts. Breuilly observes that depending on the circumstances even a culturally homogeneous people can divide on the basis of trivial cultural distinctions. Just like that a people divided by fundamental cultural distinctions can co-operate politically within the same state (Breuilly 223). Moreover, most often, the conflicts in a plural society are a part of the bargaining pressure politics.

II

Here the question that we would like to ask ourselves is how national integration should be brought about in such a situation? National integration involves a two way process. The people are enabled to accept the state as the final arbiter of their conflicts. Thus they express their loyalty to the state. The state resolves human conflicts through the institutional mechanism of its power in such a manner that it leads to consensus generation. Thus national integration process involves conflict resolution and consensus generation.

There should be no confusion about the need that the political system should be firm and tough in handling unreasonable demands. However, the system should adopt an accommodative approach as far as tackling reasonable demands are concerned. Which demand is reasonable and which one is not has to be determined by the political system itself. And to a large extend the accomplishment of a political system depends on that. The system should be firm because a nation which attains independent statehood must guard its distinct identity and be vigilant enough not to permit to lose its territorial integrity and sovereignty.

This does not mean that the system should try to assimilate the minorities to the majority. The minorities need not forgo their ethnic, cultural and linguistic characteristics. The growth and development of nationalism in an independent state does not necessarily require an erosion of primordial loyalties (Emerson 306). Even while having loyalty to primordial sentiments people can have shared positive affections toward the nation-state. Such positive affections originate out of the feeling of the people that their nation-state is just and stands for the equal benefit of all of them. This feeling is exhibited by the people through their acceptance of the state as the final judge or their disputes. Moreover, when the involved groups feel that their voice and their aspirations are given due consideration and that they have a say in the political system of the nation it helps the system to get the consensus of the groups. This two-way process of resolving conflict and generating consensus leads to strengthening the integrity of the nation. A diagrammatic representation is given below:

Techniques of National Integration

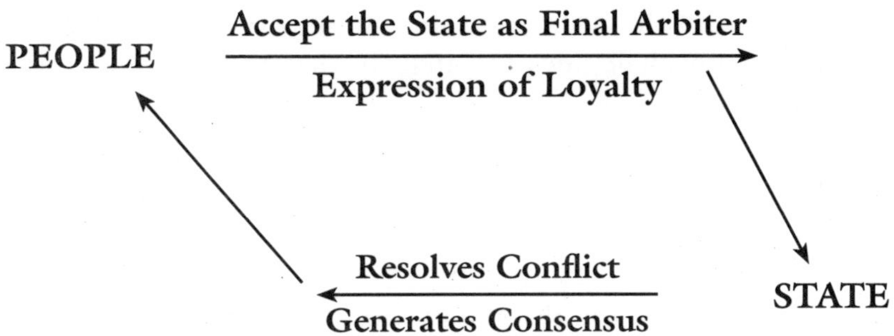

Conflicts can be resolved or minimized by adopting two methods: assimilation and accommodation. Assimilation is the process by which different groups lose their cultural and ethnic distinctness and identities, and are absorbed into the dominant group or a new group formed from the component parts (Kerina 307). Since groups have a propensity to safeguard their distinctness, official policies aimed at assimilation may lead to conflict situations. So, many plural societies prefer accommodation to assimilation. Accommodation is the process through which people belonging to different subcultures and ethnic groups can co-operate for mutual advantage in spite of differences or latent hostility. For achieving accommodation among diverse cultures and ethnic groups the sources of inter-group conflicts should be mutually adjusted. This would enable each group to enjoy reasonable freedom and security without surrendering all differences. Accommodation can be either 'informal' or 'formal'. The informal accommodation is achieved by common and non-coercive actions and agreements to alleviate stress. The formal accommodation is achieved through casting laws regulating relations among groups (Kerina 308). Consensus can be generated or increased by adopting two methods: one by adoption of positive national integration techniques and two, conflict resolution through accommodation.

III

On the basis of these theoretical premises now we would look into the major challenges to integrity that Independent India faced. For facilitating an in-depth analysis of the Indian situation I have culled out from the experience of post-Independence India three major conflicts, related to language, religion, and region, that shook the nation and which were considered by many scholars as secessionist movements that were disastrous enough to lead to the disintegration of the nation. One such issue related to language was the demand and movement for the linguistic reorganization of the country. This actually originated much before independence, affected all parts of the country and was one of the most important problems faced by the country immediately after independence.

The demand of the people of Assam to expel the 'foreign nationals' from the soil of Assam and agitation for the same was characterized by many as a challenge to Indian national unity. Involved in this struggle were questions of ethnic identity, economic imperialism of the Central Government, communal tension and language.

The unity and integrity of the nation was again put to test when the demand for an independent Sikh state of Khalistan was raised which ultimately led to the 'Bluestar Operation' of June 1984. Involved in it were issues of 'religious politics', communalism, resurgence of religious fundamentalism, politico-economic development of the region, terrorism, etc.

We would resort to a brief analysis of these three challenges, and see how these conflicts were resolved and gauge the net result.

LANGUAGE LOYALTY AND STATES REORGANISATION

The origin of the language problem in India was due to several causes. First, there is the fact of linguistic diversity as revealed by the census reports which categorise 1652 spoken languages and dialects in India. Several migrations like that of the Dravidian and Aryan races and the advent of the Turks, Iranians and Mughals as well as the English have contributed to linguistic diversity. Secondly, the agitation over the partition of Bengal starting in 1905 added a political dimension to the language problem. Thirdly, constitutional changes as envisaged in 1911, and in the Government of India Acts of 1919 and 1935 created new linguistic units. Fourthly, the Congress session of 1920 divided India into 25 linguistic units for purposes of party organization. Fifthly, the Congress resolved in 1927 to recommend creation of some linguistic provinces. Sixthly, there was a reaction against creation of linguistic states, as evident from the Dar Commission Report of 1948, which led to more agitation. Seventhly, there was the fast and death of Potti Sri Ramalu of Andhra in connection with the creation of the Andhra State which compelled the Government to yield to the demand for the creation of Andhra State. Finally, there was the States Reorganization Commission Report of 1955 followed by legislation to reorganize states.

The process started in 1956 has been continued by the creation of Tribal states in the North-East, partition of Punjab and by granting full-fledged statehood to several Union Territories.

The Colonial Rule and Language

The extension of the British Empire to India brought forth drastic changes in the linguistic scene of the country. The British depended on the traditionally literate castes for conducting the day to day administrative work. These literate castes were the upper castes of the country, mainly Brahmins.

The expanding trades and other activities of the British necessitated development of communication. Moreover, closer touch with the people was considered to be necessary for efficient administration. This led to the spread of English education and the displacement of the emphasis on Sanskrit or Persian. Selig Harrison observed correctly that when English became the common language of new national elite, India remained unified at the top and though some non-Brahmins entered these English-speaking elite, most of India continued to remain quiescent at the bottom (55). One advantage of being a member of these new elite was getting the British patronage (Mc Cully). This was followed by, what might be called, a 'Sanskritization' process, in which the lower castes followed suit.

It was mainly this English educated middle class that turned to regional languages to revolt against the orthodoxy of languages and social institutions. There was, in fact, a remarkable outburst of intellectual activity in the country. The Indian literary scene was profoundly influenced by the works of great scholars and Indologists like Max Muller, William Jones, Charles Wilkins, H.T. Colebrook etc., who translated into English the great literary and philosophical works of ancient India. The new ideas, new literary forms, methods and techniques that were acquired due to the impact of the west, were now utilised by the Indian scholars for the cultivation of vernacular literature. The growth of nationalism and the patriotic fervour created a sense of pride among Indian intellectuals and this forced them to take interest in the development of their vernacular literatures.

The Freedom Movement and Language Loyalty

An opportunity to mobilise millions of people under the unifying symbol of language for a political cause was provided by Lord Curzon's decision to partition Bengal, which was announced on July 20, 1905. The success of this agitation pointed to the fact that the Government of India was amenable to such agitations based on sentiments. Moreover, as observed by Windmiller, it did strike to many that linguistic agitation was a very powerful weapon that could be used against the foreign power. Many political leaders and linguistic groups used it to mobilise people for the national struggle for liberation. This resulted in politicising the regional linguistic unification movements (294).

Requests for redrawing of provincial boundaries on linguistic basis were presented to Edwin Montague, the Secretary of State, when he came to India in 1918. A resolution demanding the reorganisation of provinces on linguistic lines was moved in the Indian Legislative Council in the same year by B.N. Sharma, a representative from Andhra. It might have been these developments that made Montague and Chelmsford to suggest that attempt to redistribute provinces on linguistic line should be made wherever such redistributions are necessary, and can be affected by process of consent. In course of time, however, the approach of British rulers to this problem changed considerably.

The Indian National Congress and the Question of Linguistic States

The Indian National Congress took some time to understand the various dimensions of the problem. The Congress did not form a clear and sound policy regarding the question till 1920. Many of its top leaders suspected that the demand for reorganisation of the States on the basis of language was the projection of very strong sub-national tendency and provincial prejudices. The eradication of all race, creed or provincial prejudices was the declared policy of the Congress.

The Congress, however, could not withstand the pressures from the provincial Congress committees, provincial Congress leaders and the people concerned. The national leadership had to submit, gradually, to such pressures in order to strengthen and activate the provincial committees. Accordingly the Nagpur session of the Indian National Congress had passed a resolution in 1920 advocating the division of India into twenty one linguistic provinces for the administrative purpose of the party (Sitaramayya 209).

The aim of the Congress in constituting the provinces on a linguistic basis, was to break the barrier which has been created under British rule between the English-knowing classes in India and the masses, and to encourage the growth of Indian language's and the cultures associated with them (Cong.Bulletin, Feb.1956, 50).Many of the leaders of the Congress party were aware of the fact that the application of the regional languages for propagation of nationalist ideas was very successful. In 1928 the Motilal Nehru Committee appointed by the All Parties Conference considered the regrouping of the provinces on a linguistic basis as most desirable (AICC Rep. 61–69).

Gandhiji often made public his views on the question in quite unambiguous terms. For example, he wrote in the 'Harijan': "I believe that the linguistic basis is the correct basis for demarcating provinces." (Apr.1942). The Linguistic Provinces Convention which was composed of members of the Constituent Assembly, of the Central Legislature, and of the various organisations supporting the cause of linguistic and cultural redistribution of provinces recommended to the Constituent Assembly to accept the principle of linguistic and cultural redistribution of the country and set up the necessary machinery for evolving and giving effect to such a redistribution of provinces immediately after the adoption of the new Constitution and the signing of the Indo-British Treaty (Times of India Dec. 9, 1946).

Language Loyalty and States Reorganisation in Independent India

The Communal tension, the widespread confusion regarding the status of various provinces and the partition of the country marked the dawn of independence. Many of the top-ranking politicians of the country feared that just like the growth of communalism, the movement for linguistic states also would lead ultimately to the disintegration of the country. Even Gandhiji was in favour of postponing the question. Suspecting that the party in power was trying to put the issue on ice, the supporters of linguistic provinces resorted to mass struggle to focus the attention of the nation to the issue. This resulted in the appointment of the Linguistic Provinces Commission in June 1948. The Commission was in favour of postponing reorganization.

The Congress was forced to appoint the JVP Committee, which was constituted by three very outstanding figures of the party, Jawaharlal Nehru, Vallabhai Patel, and Pattabhi Sitaramayya. In its Report of 1949 there was an echo of the fears, expressed from many corners, particularly about the unity and economic growth of the country (Birla 733).

Nevertheless, the Commission stated that the case of Andhra Province should be taken up first and its implementation examined before they could think of considering the question of any other province. It was implied in these words that other provinces also would get attention if they followed suit. However, the Government did not take any step towards the formation of Andhra. But by the time of the first General Election many political parties took up the demand for linguistic states as an issue deserving immediate attention.

The Government's agreement to the formation of Andhra encouraged the various associations and groups of the other Sates to intensify their struggle for achieving reorganisation of their respective States on linguistic basis.

Nehru announced in the Lok Sabha on December 22, 1953, that the Government had set up the States Reorganization Commission. The Commission recommended the reorganization of the twenty eight States organized under the Constitution, into sixteen States and three centrally administered territories. The States Reorganisation Act came into force with effect from November 1, 1956. The demand for reorganization or the problems connected with that did not come to a close with this. There were new demands based on which new states were created later, and still there are such demands.

India could successfully solve the problem of linguistic reorganization of states. In many of the post-colonial nations such demands of the politically mobilized primordial social groups generated a feeling among many political leaders that only a suppression of these demands and the elimination of social cleavages could build the basis of stable national development. In India also, as stated earlier, the leaders were at first reluctant to concede the demand due to their fear that it would lead to the disintegration of the nation. But later, the reasonableness of the demand dawned upon them and the problem could be solved in such a way that it led to further integration of the country.

THE CITIZENSHIP CRISIS OF ASSAM

The intricacies of the problem of sub-nationalism in India are more reflected by the North Eastern states than by any other part of the country. Most of these States are very small in size and population. However, the ethnic, linguistic, religious and cultural diversity of this population is glaring. There are 116 scheduled tribes in the region. They belong to at least five different ethnic groups. Religious diversity is reflected by the presence of Hinduism, Buddhism, Islam, Christianity and certain traditional religious practices. Linguistically, the region has Assamese, Bengali, Manipuri and a variety of local languages. Economically North East is better than many Hindi speaking states like Utter Pradesh. However, the strategic location of the region and the nature of the polity, economy and society of the neighbouring regions and countries have added a set of special concerns, problems and anxieties to its normal national share. Thus the politics of this region has been deeply influenced by the influx of people from other regions as well as neighbouring countries like Myanmar and Bangladesh. A typical example is provided by the 'citizenship crisis' of Assam.

The agitation, started under the leadership of the All Assam Students Union (ASSU) and the All Assam Gana Sangram Parishad (AAGSP) in 1979 with the main demands of detection, disenfranchisement or deletion and deportation of foreigners who migrated to Assam, was resolved in August 1985. Migration has been an important contributory factor to Assam's abnormally high rate of population growth. The economic, social and political superiority achieved by the migrants over the natives was a factor that provoked the agitators. The relative economic backwardness of the State, the fear of the Assamese people of losing their identity etc., caused the agitation. The issue remained unresolved for almost six years. Talks to resolve the issue very often failed and the agitation continued for a long time.

At last, the issue got resolved in 1985. A number of factors, such as, time, the weakening of the forces of agitation, the agitators losing their hold over the people, the agitation leaders' realisation that certain demands such as the demand for the deportation of all foreigners was unattainable or that even if the Government conceded that, the actual deportation would take not only years to complete but was also virtually impossible, caused the resolution of the crisis. The Government's policy of attempting rapid economic development of the State, the desire of the new leadership of the nation to solve the issue immediately, etc., paved the way to the accord. An important aspect that is to be considered here is the nature of the agitation, whether it was anti-Indian or not. There was criticism that it was "an open movement for secession".(Ramamurthi 45) But there is lack of data to substantiate it. The agitators did not seek or receive help of any foreign nation. The agitators have no proven extra-territorial loyalty. They never demanded sovereignty or separate statehood. Thus it is clear that the agitation was not aimed at creating any anti – Indian sentiment and hence, was not anti – national. Moreover, once the problem was solved almost all the leaders and their followers expressed their willingness to come to the mainstream of Indian nationalism.

Beginnings of the foreign nationals issue

Assam began to assume much political significance during the final years of the 1970s due to the 'Foreign Nationals Issue'. Immigrants came to Assam mainly from, Bangladesh, Pakistan, Nepal, and form the various States of India. People from these places were attracted to Assam due to employment opportunities, presence of large tracts of virgin, uninhabited and fertile land, forces of circumstances such as natural and man-made calamities in their home states etc. The policy of the British Government, the Government of India and the State Government of Assam permitting the migrants to enter and stay in Assam helped the immigration.

The first few decades of the last century witnessed large scale Muslim migration into Assam from East Bengal (Present-day Bengal). Since the Muslims constituted the majority of the East Bengal peasants, who migrated into Assam the Assamese Hindu middle class, in order to create a communal balance, encouraged the Nepali people, mainly Hindus, to immigrate to Assam. Migration has affected the population growth of the State in a very serious manner.

Impact of the influx of migrants

The large scale influx of foreign nationals into Assam had its effect on the state polity. The immigrants began to assume more and more political influence in the State as their number increased and as they got themselves enrolled as voters. It posed a challenge to the emerging Assamese middle class. Both in the fields of employment and in the State politics, they thought they were not getting due share. Moreover, the pressure of population on land in the rural areas of Assam had increased much. This situation created a fear in the hearts of many that, if the continued land grabbing by the immigrants is not prevented a major section of the original inhabitants will become landless (Saikia 91). Also, it was pointed out that the pressure of population on land had affected the tribal people who practice shifting cultivation known as 'jhaming' (Saikia IJAE) The influx of immigrants had also created problems of unemployment and under-employment. As far as trade and commerce was concerned a major part of it was in the grip of immigrant settlers.

Language is a main point of controversy between the Assamese and the Bengalis. The British introduced the Bengali language as the official language of the province in 1837. Assamese children were compulsorily taught Bengali as their vernacular. It was only in 1873 that Assamese language was introduced in the schools of Assam. The furore over language attained momentum as language riots took place in Assam in 1960 when Assamese was made the official language of the State (Barua). Again in June 1972 large scale anti-Bengali riots erupted all over the Brahmaputra valley over the question of medium of instruction (Weiner 117–124). The fear of cultural and linguistic domination by the other group still persists in the minds of the Bengalis as well as the Assamese.

The immigration created a fear-psychosis among the Assamese people which was one of the main causes of the agitation. The indigenous people of Assam was alarmed by the invading swam of the land-hungry locust, which had occupied tribal blocks, grazing fields, reserved forests and the char areas of almost all the rivers of Assam. They feared that within a few decades their language and culture would be in jeopardy. So it was nothing less than the fear of losing identity.

The Assam Agitation

The demand for the detection and deportation of foreign national was one of the demands included in the twenty one-point Charter which the AASU submitted to the State Government in 1974 (AASU 15). But the demand began to assume significance only during the first half of 1979, in which year the all Assam Gana Sangram Parishad was formed to pursue the agitation. This was formed with representatives of the AASU, the Assam Sahitya Sabha and the Purbanchaliya Lok Parishad (P.L.P) Later on, the Asom Jatiyatabadi Dal, Asom Jatriyaabadi Yuva-Chatra Parishad, Asom Yuvak Samaj and a few other organizations also jointed the AAGSP.

The movement lost its non-violent character following the "drive out foreign nationals" campaign started by AASU-AAGSP. There were clashes between Bengalis and Assamese in many parts of the State. It had vast political repercussions. However, endeavours of the central government and many political leaders to solve the issue continued. The negotiations very often failed and the agitations continued for a long time.

The Assam Accord

The Assam problem was resolved by signing an accord by representatives of the Union Government and the agitation leaders at the Prime Minister's residence in New Delhi on August 15, 1985.The fourteen-point Memorandum of Settlement was a package deal including issues like constitutional safeguards for the protection and promotion of Assamese culture and language and measures for the economic and industrial development of the State. The people of Assam received the accord with much euphoria.

The agitation provided a feed-back. It had the aim of correcting the mistakes committed by various Governments since the colonial days. The political system could withstand the pressure of the agitation and it could solve the problems and extend peace and prosperity to the people and ensure their continued support. This kind of conflict resolution goes a long way in attaining national integration.

The Punjab Problem

Punjab politics since independence presents a picture of defection, opportunism, group rivalries and political horse-trading. Political, economic, social, religious and linguistic problems are intertwined to make the Punjab problem, which is the term used to connote the demand for Khalistan and connected activities, one of the most complicated and hard-to-solve problems faced by the Government of India since independence. However, it cannot be characterized as a problem created out of the divisive mentality of the people of Punjab.

Demand for Punjabi Suba

Ever since the partition of India the demand for a Punjabi-speaking state – Punjabi Subs – had dominated the politics of the region. The Akali Dal used both constitutional and agitational strategy for winning their demand for a Punjabi speaking state. The States Reorganization commission rejected the Akali demand for a Punjabi-speaking state. The Prime Minister's discussions with the Akali leadership resulted in the 'Regional Formula'. It was acceptable to the Akali Dal and hence it merged with the Congress. As a result the Akali Dal was accommodated in the Punjab Ministry. It was observed that the benefit of the merger was that it enabled the Akalis to maintain separate organizational and ethnic identities while formally they were members of a

Congress – led inter-communal coalition of Akali Sikhs, Congress Sikhs and Congress Hindus (Wallace 17).

The Akali Dal – Congress compromise was thrown to the winds, later. This was over the question of seat allotment between the Akali Dal and the Congress in the 1957 elections to the Legislative Assembly. This led to the revival of the agitation for Punjabi Suba. Based on the recommendations of the Cabinet Committee, the Parliamentary Committee and the Boundary Commission appointed by the Government, Punjab was reorganized on November 1, 1966.

Impact of the Reorganisation

The reorganization of Punjab had its impact on the social, political, economic and linguistic spheres of the State. There was considerable demographic change in Punjab due to reorganization. From a 'minority' the Sikhs became the 'majority' in the State. The Hindus are concentrated in the urban areas. In the rural areas they are scattered. The Sikhs dominate the rural areas. Moreover, they are the main land-owning class. The rural –urban differences were further increased due to the religious passions created by the reorganization (Anand 270). The economy of the State also was affected by the reorganization. With the transfer of hill areas the mineral wealth of the State went to Himachal Pradesh. The reorganization brought about considerable changes in the political arena of the State. It affected the electoral prospects of the Congress unfavourably and that of the Akali Dal favourably.

Terrorism and demand for 'Khalistan'

The factional fighting within the Akali Dal, coalition formulation with various political parties and shifting alliances of parties, religious and communal politics, the demands for autonomous status for the State, river water disputes with Haryana, factional fights within the State branch of the Congress, questions of official language, etc helped the genesis and proliferation of extremist Sikh organizations. A name often heard in the country in connection with terrorism was that of Sant Jarnail Singh Bhindranwale. He has ridden on the crest of a wave of religious revival, fanned by gnawing fear among Sikhs that they may soon be outnumbered in their home land by the Hindus. This helped the demand for 'Khalistan', a sovereign nation for the Punjabis.

The Central Government's endeavours to solve the Punjab problem in a peaceful manner failed because of the stand taken by the extremist organizations. This led to the 'Operation Bluestar', by which the terrorists fighting with the help of sophisticated weapons from within the Golden Temple were flushed out by the army, on June 2, 1984. However, the terrorist activities only mounted and it claimed the life of no less a figure than the Prime Minister, Indira Gandhi, who was assassinated on October 31, 1964 by her Sikh bodyguard. This was followed by large scale anti-Sikh rioting in Delhi. It was in such a confused situation that Rajiv Gandhi became Prime Minister. He could sign, after much discussions, the Punjab Peace Accord with the Akali Dal president, Longowal on July 24, 1965.

The Peace Accord envisaged the transfer of Chandigarh to Punjab and certain Hindi-speaking areas (to be determined by a Commission) to Haryana, rehabilitation of those army personnel who deserted in the wake of the 'operation blue star', reference of those portions of the Anandapur Sahib resolution which dealt with Centre-State relations to the Sarkaria Commission, and reference of the claims of Punjab and Haryana to Ravi –Beas waters to a tribunal.

This did not bring an end to all the woes of the state. Nevertheless, it helped a lot along with the Prime Minister's package to Punjab, announced on March 3, 1989, to start normalization process in Punjab.

Basically the Punjab problem was not religious or cultural separatism as the Sikh religion was until the beginning of the twentieth century considered a reformist group of Hinduism. There is also social and cultural identification with the Hindus and very frequent intermarriages. Punjabi sub-nationalism is built around the politics of Sikh religion. This politics has not become identified with the politics of the Congress, which is based on secularism and Indian nationalism. From the beginning of independence Sikh politics became anti-Congress and as it was based on religion, was unable to prevent its capture by extremists. Terrorism is only a manifestation of Sikh political extremism.

As Robert L.Hardgrave, Jr. observes, the exclusion of the Akalis from power is the main political issue involved in the Punjab problem. The Akali politicians' craze for power has led them at one time to split the original Akali Dal into eight factions. The factional fights of the Akalis also helped the spread of terrorism. There is ample proof to substantiate the fact that it was with the assistance and connivance of certain foreign countries that terrorism became widespread in the State. Terrorism is a global phenomenon, and in Punjab only a minority was indulging in it.

Now it can be safely concluded that the 'Punjab problem' was nothing more than a sub-national movement. An analysis of the various aspects of the problem shows that, though sometimes a minority demanded the establishment of a separate nation, the majority was always against it. The latter's demands included more autonomy, more economic opportunity and more respect to the Punjabi religion and language. When compared to the other States of India, the people of Punjab formed an affluent society. Their expectations for more agricultural and industrial development and more employment opportunity for their industrious and hard working youth could not be realized to their satisfaction. Neither the State Government nor the political parties of the State were ready to take the responsibility. They, instead, vied with one another in blaming the other. The Central Government also was blamed for putting hurdles in the path of the State's economic development. Nevertheless, when the problem was finally solved even the extremists joined the mainstream and thus imparted much more integrity and development to the Indian nation.

IV

CONCLUSION

It has been observed that India possesses problems due to its size, cultural and ideological diversity and regionalism and that Indian Government and politics emerge from this mosaic of overlapping influences, unable to function without due regard for the impact of each (Park 7). However, the operation of the political system transforms these influences into creative nation-building forces due to its capacity to accommodate variety and multiplicity. A plural society's ability to accommodate divergent interests within the framework of a larger unity helps the national integration process. India has fashioned for herself a democratic system with a federal structure, a representative government, universal adult suffrage, free elections, the rule of law, an independent judiciary, and fundamental rights. The nation's tradition of respecting all religious faiths is continued after independence by subscribing to the concept of the secular state. The process of economic planning has led to the augmented financial and economic integration of the nation. The country can boast of an efficient system of mass communication, provisions for minority safeguards, and a commitment to secure cent per cent literacy.

The Constitution, the Government and the political parties recognise the diversity of India. The people and their leaders regard cultural diversity as a natural condition to be respected and safeguarded. That the political leadership of the country is aware about this is clear from the words of the former Prime Minister, Rajiv Gandhi, "We are consciously preserving the traditional characteristics of our regional cultures. No group faces the prospect of being forced into any fixed mould. No group experiences the feeling that its safety and progress will be promoted only by casting off its cultural or other identity and getting itself 'assimilated' into some larger whole." (5). About the time – tested sense of unity of the people of India, Jawaharlal Nehru wrote: "Some kind of a dream of unity has occupied the mind of India since the dawn of civilization. That unity was not conceived as something imposed from outside, a standardisation of externals or even of beliefs. It was something deeper within its fold, the widest tolerance of belief and custom was practiced and every variety acknowledged and even encouraged.... at almost any time in recorded history an Indian would have felt more or less at home in any part of India." (Govt.). Eminent political scientists have observed that in India, there is no direct or hidden domination of any single ethnic or religious group (Brass 14–16).

It should be in the light of these facts that the cultural diversity and the sub-national demands of independent India be viewed. The cultural and religious renaissance in the country during the pre-independence period resulted not only in the promotion of Indian nationalism but it also sowed the seeds of sub-nationalism. Many factors like the development of the regional languages and democratization of political life contributed to the promotion of sub-nationalism (Nayar 8). Often an appeal to sub-national identity is aimed at altering the nature of the distribution of resources. To effect a change in the distribution of resources, an appeal to sub-national identity can seek three ways (Breuilly 224). Firstly, it can be a method of attaining a more favourable position in central government and gaining a better role in its decision making. Accordingly, groups may bring to the attention of the central government their under representation in the distribution of development projects or educational facilities. Secondly, a group can try to reduce the power of the central government through devices such as a federal constitution and entrenched legal rights. Thirdly, a group may demand total independence, may be as a further extension of the second position. So, "ethnicity, language or any other criteria used to underpin a claim to sub-national identity can, therefore, be understood as a political resource." (Breuilly 225).

After independence India had to confront sub-national movements in a few places. But endeavours aimed at national integration helped the political solution of these and bring the people of these places to the national mainstream. In the present work three important problems related to sub-national loyalties were studied in detail. These were three major conflicts related to the people's loyalty to language, religion and region, that have challenged the strength of Indian nationalism since independence. As explained earlier many people including Jawaharlal Nehru, were afraid that demands based on the language loyalty of the people of India was capable enough to challenge the unity of India. But time proved that their fears were baseless. It took some time for the political leadership of the nation to learn that this demand was a reasonable one and not secessionist. The reorganisation of states mainly on linguistic lines led to successful conflict resolution. Here, the people's acceptance of the State as the ultimate arbiter of their affairs was clear. So this demand cannot be termed as separatist. The States reorganisation had, in fact, enabled all sections of the population to participate in the Government of the country by overcoming linguistic barriers. Thus, the reorganisation promoted the unity of India.

The citizenship crisis of Assam, as we have seen, was not one precipitated by fissiparous tendencies. The people of Assam turned to the Central Government for correcting the wrongs done to them by various governments that came into power in Delhi since the time of the Colonial rule. The accommodative tactics applied by the Central Government for conflict resolution was successful. Though the regional party that projected the Assamese sub-nationalism came into power in the State, following the signing of the Assam accord, the people rejected it in the next general election and voted for a Congress (I) Government. As explained earlier, this was a vote against separatism and violence.

The religious, ethnic and linguistic criteria used by the Sikhs of Punjab to substantiate a claim to sub-national identity were, political resources. It is in order to effect a change in the distribution of resources, including political power that the Sikhs appealed to sub-national loyalty. But a minority, with the connivance of certain foreign countries made use of this opportunity to undermine the integrity of India. Many factors such as the geographical setting of the region, the growth of religious fundamentalism, etc., made the State vulnerable to such foreign influences. But, as made clear earlier, the terrorists and their secessionist demands were not supported by the majority of the population of Punjab. In fact, the majority has shunned terrorism and expressed the desire to be in the national mainstream.

These studies point towards certain facts. Firstly, in post-independence India nationalism has become a stronger force than sub-nationalism which is the creation of primordial sentiments. Secondly, it was the people's desire to live together and maintain their state that was expressed through their acceptance of the state as the final arbiter in the case of states reorganisation, the Assam agitation and the Punjab problem. Thirdly, in all these cases the politico-economic system helped to resolve the conflicts by adopting the method of accommodation. On many occasions the people have expressed their approval of the state's approach to conflict resolution. Surely, this is the reason why the people turn more and more to the State for conflict resolution. Lastly, in India, people can have a belief in linguistic, religious or regional sub-nationalism and an Indian nationalism at the same time (Sreekumar 191–214).

There are many factors that prevent sub-nationalism from becoming secessionism in India. The most important factor is the fundamental unity of India about which volumes have been written (Mookerji). Another one is contributed by the deliberate and planned measures aimed at national integration pursued by the political system of the nation with the help of a written Constitution and a functioning democratic political party system. The political system is fashioned in such a way that it can accommodate variety and multiplicity. People's involvement as well as faith in the political system is another factor that integrates and strengthens the nation. This is explained by the tremendous popular-participation in the democratic process. Yet another factor is the political economy of the nation. Rapid economic development especially since 1991 has created a large middle class with a stake in Indian unity. People are now hopeful that "...India might have a more stable, peaceful, and negotiated transition into the future than, say, China." (Das xix).

The nature of the political leadership is another factor that deserves mentioning. While in many states the leadership is unstable, at the national level there has been the tradition of strong leadership. The plural nature of the Indian society has a very important role in preventing sub-nationalism from becoming secessionism. While at the national level India is a federal society in which language groups and religious minorities have an important role, each state is a plural society in which castes and communal groups play a political role (Nayar, 1966, 93). Many unilingual states are plural in many other ways. Actually, not even a single State is cent per cent unilingual. Linguistic and religious overlapping is quite common. These are some of the factors that make sub-nationalism a weaker political force than Indian nationalism. Apart from these there are many other integrating forces in India such as the educational system, the introduction of modern technology and the important role of the communication media. In spite of the language barriers the educational system tends to unify the country by subjecting the students to a process of socialisation. The media such as television and radio are powerful instruments of integration. Though the regional news papers may sometimes support secessionist demands the press, taken as a whole, has been a powerful agent of unification by compelling the country to think in terms of the nation.

India today is a unified, strong and vibrant nation. It is evoking an 'intense belief' in its future in the minds of many like Nandan Nilekani, who writes, "I still think that after a long and convoluted path, after many a stumble and wrong turn, a different kind of moment seems to be upon us. For the first time, there is a sense of hope across the country, which I believe is universal. There is a momentum for change, evident in the enthusiasm of our younger legislators, the mushrooming of civil society organizations, and activists fighting in the courts for reforms in Governance and for the protection of fundamental rights" (484). These fighting in the courts even for reforms in governance are testimony to the fact that people consider their State just and hence the final judge of their affairs. This in turn is thanks to the political process of accommodation of diversity that the political system is pursuing and which makes national integration a meaningful and continuous process in India. There is no doubt that Indian policy makers took very shrewd measures in the past for solving societal conflicts. However, it is my vehement hope that, policy formulators of tomorrow may have a lesson or two to learn from this paper and that would enable them to give due consideration to the multicultural nature of Indian society, the nature of conflicts emanating due to that and the need for adopting such conflict resolution techniques that may help the process of national integration.

REERENCES

All Assam Students Union. Memorandum to the Prime Minister of India on Problem of Foreign Nationals in Assam. Guwahati. n.d.

All India Congress Committee, All Parties Conference. 1928, Report of the Motilal Nehru Committee. Allahabad: 1928.

Anand, J.C. "Politics of Retreating Communalism", (ed.), State Politics in India.Ed. Iqbal Narain. Meerut: 1976.

Barua,Bhaben.Language and the National Question in Northeast India. Guwahati. 1972.

Birla, G.D. "The Economic Conditions of India". The Asiatic Review. XLV. 164.

Brass, Paul. Religion, Language and Politics in North India. Delhi: 1975.

Breuilly, John. Nationalism and the State. Manchester: 1982.

Congress Bulletin. New Delhi: February. 1956.

Das, Gurcharan. India Unbound : From Independence to Global Information Age. Penguin Books. New Delhi: 2007.

Emerson, Rupert. "Paradoxes or Asian Nationalism", Far Eastern Quarterly. 1.1. (1954).

Emerson, Rupert. "Post-Independence Nationalism in South and Southeast Asia: A Reconsideration". Pacific Affairs XLIV.2 (1971).

Emerson, Rupert. "The Problem of Identity, Statehood and Image in the New nations: The situations in Africa". Comparative Politics. (April 1969).

Gandhi, Rajiv. A Changing India in a Changing World. Ministry of Information and Broadcasting. Government of India. New Delhi: 1985.

Government ofIndia. Ministry ofInformation and Broadcasting. One Country One People. New Delhi: 1986.

Harijan. 19 April 1942.

Harrison, Selig. S. India: The Most Dangerous Decades. Madras: Oxford University Press.1960.

londansky, V. The Impasses and Prospects of Tropical Africa Moscow: 1970.

Kerina, Mburbumba . "Plural Societies and the Application of Democracy". (ed), Intergroup Accommodation in Plural Societies .Ed. Nic Rhoodie. London: 1978.

McCully, Bruce. English Education and the Origins of Indian Nationalism Massachusetts: 1966.

Mookerji, Radha Kumud. Fundamental Unity of India. Bharatiya Vidya Bhavan. Bombay: 1970.

Navari, Comelia. "The Origins of the Nation-state". The Nation State: The Formation of Modern Politics. Ed. Leonard Tivey. Oxford: 1981.

Nilekani, Nandan. Imaging India: Ideas for the New Century. Penguin. New Delhi: 2008.

Park, Richard L., and Bruce de Mesquita. India's Political System. New Jersey: 1979.

Ramamurthi, P. Real Face of the Assam Agitation. New Delhi: 1980.

Saikia, P.D. "Problems of Agricultural Development in the Tribal Areas of Northeast India". Indian Journal of Agricultural Economics. XXX. 3. 1970.

Sitaramayya, Pattabhi. A History of The Indian National Congress. Bomby: 1946.

Smith, Anthony D. The Ethnic Revival .Cambridge: 1981.

Smith, Anthony D. Theories of Nationalism. London: 1971.

Sreekumar,K.C."TheoreticalDimensionsofPost-Independence Nationalism". ISDA Journal. 7.2 & 3.1997.

Sukumaran Nayar, V.K. "Indian Nationalism (in the context of sub—nationalism and communalism)", Paper presented in the All India Nehru Centenary Seminar. (Mimeographed). Trivandrum: 1989.

Sukumsran Nayar, V.K. "New challenges Before Indian Federalism". Kerala Journal of Political Studies. 1.1. 1966.

Sumoniya, Nodary, "Nationalism and Political Struggle in the Newly-Free countries". The Evolution of Nationalism in Asia and Africa. Moscow: U.S.S.R. Academy of Sciences, 1970.

Times of India. Bombay. 9 December. 1946.

Tinker, Hugh . "The Nation State in Asia". The Nation State: The Formation of Modern Politics. Ed. Leonard Tivey. Oxford: 1981.

Wallace, Paul. "Religious and Secular Politics in Punjab: The Sikh Dilemma in Competing Political System". Punjab Journal of Politics. V.1, 1981.

Weiner,Myron.Sons of the Soil: Migration and Ethnic Conflict in India. Princeton: 1978.

Windmiller, Marshall. "Linguistic Regionalism in India". Pacific Affairs. xxvii. 4. 1954.

5

Casteism: Threat to National Integration

Anil Kumar Verma

National integration in India is usually taken as synonymous with communal harmony, and perhaps rightly so because of the background of religious frenzy leading to communal violence that defined the birth of India as a nation. Communal harmony must continue to engage us as we are far away from the goal of national integration so important for establishing peaceful, prosperous and progressive India. However, national integration is a multi-dimensional concept. In our enthusiasm for communal harmony, some more and equally compelling aspects to national integration viz. casteism, regionalism, linguism and narrow mindedness etc. have not been adequately discussed in the framework of national integration. This allowed many of them to assume disturbing dimensions. One of them i.e. casteism assumed a proportion unimaginable in Indian society and polity; caste overtook everything else as an instrument of effective political mobilisation, bureaucratic functioning and control, economic activities, and even social intercourse. That dented the 'rule of law' by giving primacy to caste-relations over law; that also affected adversely the quality of individual and community relations by private and public demonstrations of caste discriminations. Thus, casteism seeped into all aspects of Indian society like termites eating into the vitals of internal cohesion that is the hallmark of Indian society.

In this essay, we argue that casteism is no less a threat to national integration than communalism. There are caste divisions and dissensions within a religious group that are no less detrimental to the social fabric than the communal disharmony.

In fact, caste tensions, often resulting in caste conflicts, diminish the quality of day-to-day social life by perpetuating both visible and invisible violence and discrimination in interpersonal relations within a community. While communal tensions find occasional outbursts that give them greater publicity, caste tensions and conflicts are a regular and day-to-day phenomenon that is taken as fait accompli. We often try to hide caste tensions and conflicts within the grand narrative of communalism where we try to position a religious community as united, homogenised and singularly positioned vis-à-vis another religious community. That is a double treachery because in doing so we try to give a wrong signal that – one, all is well within a religious community; and, two, a religious community as a whole is conflictually positioned against another religious community.

The communal angle to national integration divides Indian society into two broad meta-religious identities viz. Hindus and Muslims, and tries to workout amity and goodwill between them. But, the caste angle to national integration transcends these meta-religious identities and looks at the several micro-identities of which they are made of. This is because castes and casteism are not confined to Hindus alone; Muslims too are neck deep into it. Even the Sikhs and Christians have been facing this problem in one form or the other. Thus, the major religious formations in India (Hindu, Muslim, Sikh, Christian) have all been facing casteism that tends to sow the seeds of differences, conflicts and hatred within each religious denomination. While communalism brings distancing between and among religious communities, casteism brings distancing among the members of one religious community. Hence, casteism is simply an extension of communalism; or we may say that casteism is simply communalism within one religious community. Alam(1999) puts it very succinctly "... casteism has been a source of enormous strength to communalism..."

Debate on national integration had always been within a restricted domain of communalism. The dynamics of contemporary national integration has to be sought in economic, political and social realities of modern India. The predominant discourse on communalism of Hindu-Muslim variety distracts from the larger discourse of class oriented society where downtrodden and marginalised of both the communities are prevented from coming together. Hence, casteism and communalism both breed exclusion, hallmark of a nation that may not be adequately integrated.

CASTEISM: A COMMON DENOMINATOR IN MAJOR RELIGIONS

Whenever we talk about caste and casteism, the main focus is on one religious community i.e. Hindus. There are several reasons for that. One, there is major share of Hindus in the population of Indian society; two, the Hindus have been the original inhabitants here, and other religions came only subsequently; three, the caste hierarchy and caste discrimination have been so ingrained in the Hindu social order that the entire discourse in social sciences have centred around untouchability, forward and backward castes, and OBCs and Dalits. The caste and caste system percolated in Islam and Christianity owing to the act of conversions by Muslim Rulers during the medieval period and the Church in modern times respectively. That is why, is spite of the two religions (Islam and Christianity) professing social equality, we find caste hierarchy and consequent caste discrimination in both Islam and Christianity. The issues of dalit Christians and that of 'pasmanda' Muslims have recently acquired great public attention.

Casteism in Islam

The story of how casteism crept into Indian Islam is ingrained into how Islam came to India. It is said that soon after the death of the Prophet, a group of 20 Muslims, arrived in 643 AD in

Kerala to preach Islam, founded the first Indian mosque at Kodungallur, in todays Thrissur district, nearly a century before the first arrival in India in 711 AD of a Muslim conqueror, Muhammed bin Qasim. While the role of political patronage and post conquest coercions may not be denied in the spread of Islam, several studies point that traditionally disadvantaged and deprived sections of Indian society moved to Islam to escape the miseries of caste discriminations (Krishnan: 2010). Even Swami Vivekananda (1897) lend credence to this, "The Mohammedan conquest of India came as a salvation to the downtrodden, to the poor. That is why one-fifth of our people have become Mohammedans. It was not the sword that did it all. It would be the height of madness to think it was all the work of sword and fire"

Islam has an egalitarian social ideology upholding equality and fraternity. With this ideology, it challenged the traditional hierarchy of Arab society. It was with this altered state of social organisation that Islam came to north India in the 12th century. At that time India had already developed its own form of social stratification known as the caste system (Krishnan: 2010).

The Census Report 1901 for Bengal records the existence of three social divisions recognised by Muslims, viz. Ashraf, the "noble", which includes all undoubted descendants of foreigners and converts from "upper" caste Hindus; Ajlaf, the "mean people", which includes all "occupational" groups and converts of "lower" ranks; and, in some places, Arzal, the "lowest of all", with connotation similar to the "Chandal" among Hindus and with whom other Muslims will not associate and who are forbidden entry into the mosque and use of public burial grounds. The census 1901 lists castes under each division with a social precedence as among the Hindus (Krishnan: 2010).

Many Muslim scholars (Ansari: 1959, Imtiaz: 1973) have accepted this division of Muslims in India into ashraf (noble born), ajlaf (mean and lowly) and arzal (excluded). Ansari suggests that each of these categories was further divided into a number of groups which can be called as castes. Later Imtiaz (1973) argued that in terms of day-to-day social interactions the arzal existed on the margins of society. They engaged in the lowly occupation of scavenging, confined their marriages within the group and were excluded in the villages as well as the towns into separate residential quarters in which members of the other categories did not live. Kader (2004) points that Muslim community needs to realise that caste stratification, howsoever blasphemous, is a reality of the Muslim society in India.

The Census Commissioner of 1931 JH Hutton also observed that neither the followers of Islam nor of Christianity could escape the infection of caste; even the change of religion does not destroy the caste system, for Muslims who do not recognise it as valid, are found to observe it in practice(Krishnan: 2010).

It is usually argued that Islam does not permit inequality and prohibits discrimination on the ground of birth etc. On whether Islam disapproves social stratification, Imtiaz (2009) suggests that the opinion is divided on this. Some (Lindholm: 1965) argue that Islam was against any social stratification and posited the inherent equality of all human beings tended to represent the presence of arzal communities as merely an occupational division without any status implications. From their point of view, the disabilities and exclusion characterizing the arzal communities applied to individuals and were relevant only in the occupational realm. Once their members move outside the occupational realm they are at par with everyone else. Others (Husnain: 2005) did not take the position that Islam was against social stratification. They viewed the existence of arzal communities as reflecting a system in which groups were ranked as superior and inferior and individuals carried the burden of their group status through having to suffer disabilities and exclusion as members of groups. Husnain (2005) writes, "It is true that the egalitarian social order of Islam stands in sharp contrast with the ideology of caste yet the 'Indian Islam' and 'Hindu Caste System' has been able to achieve a substantial compatibility". Though Islam accepts differentiation based on gender and tribe, it does not recognise social stratification. But in reality, the Muslim community remains diversified, fragmented and as caste-ridden as any other community of India (Alam, 2003: 4881).

Islam may not discriminate between people but Muslims do. Muslims with higher status do not allow dalit Muslims to come forward or improve their working or living status....In the Constituent Assembly, "during decision on reservation for minorities it was suggested by Sardar Vallabhbhai Patel and Dr. Ambedhkar that even Muslims include dalits in the same fashion that Hindu do and changing ones caste does not improve his social and financial status. Therefore even Muslims dalits should be provided with reservation. This suggestion was opposed by five Muslim members of the committee saying Muslims do not need reservation on the basis of their religion... Tara Singh struggled to extend the reservation to Sikh dalits and he was successful in 1956. Buddhists were also given reservations and this work was accomplished by V. P. Singh in 1990. Following their footsteps, even dalit Muslims have formed Pasmanda Front which is working to include dalit Muslims in scheduled caste (Ansari: 2009)".

Writing about Bihar Muslims, Papaya Ghosh (Bhaumik: 1992) says that the major dichotomy in Bihar is represented by lower caste 'rasils' and upper caste 'sharif'. While 'rasils' included lower caste artisans and the 'jolahas, the sharifs' included the sayyeds, sheikhs and upper strata of Muslim society. In early twentieth century, lower caste Muslims grouped themselves as jolahas or momins. That divide was visible throughout the national movement.

In a study about Hyderabad Muslims, Ali (2002) writes that Muslims usually come in two social categories: higher castes (Syed, Sheikh, Pathan, and Mughal) and lower or service castes (Qureshi or Qassab/butchers, and Ladaf/cotton beaters). The high castes claim foreign origin from Saudi Arabia, Iran, Afghanistan, or Central Asia, while the members of the low castes are low-caste Hindu converts. However, some high caste Muslims viz. Pathans and Sheikhs may also be Hindu converts (Ali: 2002).

During Freedom Struggle, the Muslim League tried to attempt Muslim unity and mobilise Muslims on a common platform. But the upper class Muslims tried to distance themselves from momins. That generated tensions between the 'sharifs' and the 'momins' as the upper castes Muslims, though in minority, dominated the League. The momin leadership initially clashed with the League on class issues among the Muslim. However after the mid-1930s the momins concentrated more on seeking greater representation in legislative bodies by stressing on their backwardness. Ghosh pointed out that during this phase the earlier class contradictions between upper caste Muslims and Momins gave way to the quest for greater representation in the assembly (Bhaumik: 1992)

Muslim community is usually projected as a homogenised block in secular-communal discourse. The fact is otherwise. The community faces a triple divide; one, it is divided between broad sects viz. Shia-Sunnis-Ahmedia; two, each sect is further sub-divided on class lines that Ghosh calls 'sharifs' and 'momins' or what Alam (1999) calls 'masses' and 'gentry'; three, the community also faces hierarchical social stratification in the form of caste divisions of which pasmanda Muslims (dalit and backward Muslims) are burning example.

Highlighting the class divide, Alam (1999) points out that Muslims are split between 'masses' and the 'gentry'; the latter always assuming the leadership. The common Muslim finds disconnect between him and the leadership. Alam further says, "... a Shafique Ahmed can surely become a governor but is in no position to even win a municipal election from a Muslim constituency". Though Alam tries to give a class orientation to the Muslim society by positioning the upper class Muslims vis-à-vis the downtrodden Muslims, yet what he does not write is indicative of the caste connections between lower caste Hindus and lower class Muslims. Writing at the end of the decade of Nineties, Alam (1999) said:

> "An ordinary Muslim would rather vote for a yadav or kurmi put up by Mulayam Singh or Laloo Yadav than to one from their own upper classes... Ordinary Muslim masses find these communities of OBCs and dalits as placed adjacent to them and not in a relationship of dependence...it is a case of alignment of interests of a secular nature, a social coalition of oppressed forces".

But, what Alam ignored is the act of conversion of the lower caste Hindus to Islam, and that many among the lower class Muslims still reminisce their old 'Hindu connections'. In fact, some Muslim organisations had appealed to the S. Court (writ petition no. 13 of 2008) challenging as discriminatory para 3 of the Constitution (Scheduled caste) Order, 1950 issued by the President of India under Art.341 of the Constitution of India on the ground that certain Hindu castes were declared as the SCs whereas their Muslim counterparts were discriminated and denied the status of SCs. They espoused the cause of 'dalit Muslims' who were deprived of the status of SC on the ground that there is no caste system in egalitarian Islam. They argued that the uncomfortable reality is that the Indian Muslim social milieu is caste based not scripturally but practically. The petitioner, a Khatik organisation from Maharashtra, further argued:

> "...historically speaking, there was only one caste of Khatiks. Later on, some of them converted to Islam and became Muslim Khatiks. Even their names carry the surname of Khatik. Sometimes, the names are such that it is difficult to distinguish between a Hindu Khatik and a Muslim Khatik. Muslims Khatiks etc are as educationally, socially and economically backward as the Hindu Khatiks but they have not been declared as the khatik Scheduled Casts. Likewise, Muslim Mehtars/HalalKhor/Lal Begi/Bhangi/Muslim/Dhobi, Mukri, Garudi and Mochi etc. have been denied the status of scheduled castes whereas their Hindu counterparts have been enjoying the benefits and privileges granted to the Scheduled

> Castes... Actually, the categorization of Dalits as Hindu Dalits, Christian Dalits, Muslim Dalits, Sikh Dalits or Buddist Dalit is a recent phenomenon...Earlier, they were known as "depressed classes".

There is a consensus among scholars that most Indian Muslims are descendants of 'untouchable' and 'low' caste converts, with only a small minority tracing their origins to Arab, Iranian and Central Asian settlers (Sikand, 2003). Muslims who claim foreign descent assert a superior status for themselves as ashraf or 'noble'. Descendants of indigenous converts are, on the other hand, commonly referred to contemptuously as ajlaf or 'base' or 'lowly' (Zainuddin, 2003). Going by this classification, an overwhelming 75% of Muslim population of India would fall into the ajlaf category (Anwar, 2001). But conversion to the egalitarian faith of Islam has not helped their cause. The ajlaf continue to be discriminated against by the Muslim upper caste (Sahay, 2003). The ill treatment meted out to the lower and backward caste Muslims has led to a movement for recognition of the lower caste Muslims or 'Dalit Muslims' as Scheduled Castes, on par with the lower castes in the Hindu society (Sikand, 2003).

Kader (2004) resents the caste debate among Muslims and puts a note of caution for the community as a whole: "Aren't schisms based on Shia-Sunni, Deobandi, Barelwi, Ahl-i-Hadith, Jamaat-i-Islami etc. enough that we are now seeking to create categories like 'dalit Muslim' and 'forward caste Muslim?... A duplication of the social stratification based on caste being practised by the Hindu community of India, is the last thing that the Muslims of India need."

However, the ground reality, whether we like or not, is that social stratification is a hard fact of Indian Muslim society and such social categories as Backward Muslims and Dalit Muslims are now fast taking shape. This can also be gauged from the list of state-wise backward castes drawn by Backward Class Commission. Almost in every state, we find several Muslim castes included in the list of OBCs, a status that entitles them for affirmative action benefits mainly reservations in state services and educational institutions. This can be checked from the Central List of OBCs put up by the National Commission for Backward Classes for each state on its website that lists backward Muslim castes in that state.1 Thus, the recognition of certain caste/categories from Muslim community as backward castes/ categories have been long accepted, and that bracketed them with the backward castes from Hindu community. Similarly, there are several castes/categories among Muslims who are not only agitating, but also fighting legal battle for recognition of their dalit status.

CASTEISM IN CHRISTIANITY

Caste is an important variable of social structure in Hindu society. With the advent of the Christian missionaries in India, proselytisation began. The missionaries tried to convert low caste Hindus who were hit by caste prejudice. These missionaries, concentrating on tribals, persuaded them to believe that they were not Hindus, and Christianity, an alien religion, was their own and that Jesus Christ was also a 'dalit'. In their desire to lead a life of respect, many low caste Hindus and tribals got converted to Christianity.

Unfortunately, Christianity in India is not free from the caste bias. Christians practise discrimination based on casteism in Churches in spite of the fact that approximately 75% of Christians are 'dalits'. In most of the churches, Christians of upper caste occupy the central part, while the Dalits are assigned to the wings. The Dalits were to take communion only after the upper caste people had done so [EPW: 1989].

In the Indian Catholic Church, both in the hierarchy and in the structure, Dalit Christians have no place at all. Out of 156 Catholic bishops in India, 150 bishops belong to the upper caste community. Only 6 bishops belong to dalit community. Out of

12,500 Catholic priests, only 600 are from dalit community. In a country where job opportunities are scarce and highly competitive, most of the job opportunities within church-run educational and other institutions go in favor of the upper caste people.

Christian Dalits forming majority of the Christian population of India were denied recognition as SCs under the Presidential Order of 1950. The assumption behind this was that once converted to Christianity, SC/STs no longer face any economic or social discrimination to deserve special protection from the state. This is however far from the truth. Despite universalism as preached in Christianity, the Christian clergy from the upper-caste background dominate the churches and practise discrimination against the Christian Dalits. Separate places in pews, separate hearse and burial grounds, less than five per cent inter-caste marriages, segregated churches, caste titles in name boards and in church and secular documents are some of the most blatant forms of discrimination. As the Christian Dalits are becoming more assertive about their rights-both as Christians within the community, and as a part of the exploited poor outside, Catholic priests fear that that the church is losing youth to Marxism. These bishops are now trying to purge their dioceses of priests who (inspired by the 'liberation theology' in which Marxian analysis is an important component) have been involved in, and often have been leading, people's struggles [EPW: 1989].

Voicing the same concern, the Archbishop George Zur, Apostolic Pro-Nuncio to India said while inaugurating the Catholic Bishops Conference of India in 1991:

> "Though Catholics of the lower caste and tribes form 60 per cent of Church membership they have no place in decision-making. Scheduled caste converts are treated as lower caste not only by high caste Hindus but by high caste Christians too. In rural areas they cannot own or rent houses, however well-placed they may be. Separate places are marked out for them in the parish churches and burial grounds".

Recently in January 2011, tension mounted in a predominantly Christian village Thachur, near Chennai when upper caste Catholic Christians opposed the burial of dalit catholic priest in the cemetery marked for upper caste Christians. The village population comprised of Reddiars, migrants from Andhra Pradesh, and Dalits, including Adi Dravidars and Arunthathiars – all of them are Christian converts. The village has three cemeteries; one inside the church complex is claimed by the upper caste Reddiars, while the dalit Christians have theirs on the outskirts of the village. Such instances can be multiplied (Dorairaj: 2011).

The dalit Christians, especially of the catholic sect, have been agitating for long against the caste discrimination practised within their community and the church. They have been demanding the extension of constitutional privileges allotted to the SC and the ST communities belonging to Hindu, Sikh and Buddhist fold. Of late, the higher echelons of the Catholic Church have shown interest in this matter by espousing the demand for reservation though evading its responsibility of eliminating casteism within Christianity. [EPW: 1995, p. 3041].

Logically, the term 'Dalit Christians' is self-contradictory. How can a person be a 'Dalit' when he is a Christian? Christianity does not recognise any caste system. When a person gets converted, he is no longer a Hindu and thus does not fall into any category of the caste hierarchy. There is in fact twice-alienation of Dalit Christians; one, they are discrimination within the Church, two; they are discrimination by the State. The former treats them unfavourably; the later does not bring them within the canopy of affirmative action policies.

CASTEISM IN SIKHISM

There is no place for casteism in Sikhism too. The rejection of the caste system by Guru Nanak, the first Guru of the Sikhs, appeared categorical when he founded the Sikh religion in

15 century. One of the widely quoted of his 'sabads is': Fakar jati phakar nau, Sabhana jia ika chau (Worthless is caste and worthless an exalted name; for all mankind, there is but single refuge).

When the Sikh leadership chose to assert a separate and distinct identity to underline their boundary demarcation from the Hindus, they tried to focus on their rejection of 'varnashram system' and purity-pollution syndrome prevalent in Hinduism. Consequently, many dalits converted to Sikh religion with a view to improving their social status. Yet, the real picture in the present society is that there is still a wide gap between the principles of Sikhism and social practices; the sikh society lacks social homogenisation and the relics of caste hierarchy inherited from the Hindu society continue unabated.

Some scholars like Grewal confirm this and offer a justification too. He opines that Guru Nanak's rejection of caste, as also his conception of equality, is in terms of religious criterion; he does not conceive of equality in social and economic terms. Practices such as 'sangat' and 'langar' brought equality in religious gatherings and ensured eating of food by all, high or low, together; the 'karah prasad' was another that included prasad offered by one and all, including those from low castes, deposited in a single pot and distributed to everyone as 'holy pradas' (Grewal: 1972). So, in religious congregations, there was no scope for discrimination on the basis of social or economic status.

When Guru Gobind Singh initiated Khalsa brotherhood in 1699, all the first five initiates (panj pyare) came from the lower castes. As per the command of the 10th Guru, there was to be no living Guru; the holy book 'Guru Granth Sahib' containing compositions of a number of saints such as Sheikh Farid, Kabir (weaver) and Ravidas (chamar) was to be the only Guru.

As all the Ten Sikh Gurus came from kharti caste, the early Sikh following was from khatris. However, there was massive entry of the jats from the time of the sixth Guru that changed caste equations within Sikhism. In the 1881 Census, the jats, who dominated rural Panjab, constituted 63% of the entire Sikhs (Puri: 2003). "Every Sikh was equal in the presence of the Granth Sahib, in the sangat and the langar, but in the life outside, social differences were legitimised" (Grewal 1994:118). There was a divide between the Sikh nobility and the common Sikhs. The Sikhs displayed caste hierarchy and discrimination against the untouchables who were denied access to villages, public wells and Gurdwaras (Pratap Singh 1933:146, quoted by Puri: 2003)

IMPLICATIONS OF CASTEISM FOR NATIONAL INTEGRATION

We have discussed, in brief, how caste and casteism engulfed not only the Hindus, but also the Muslims, Sikhs and Christians. This has actually taken communalism down the stream in society, and affected adversely individual relations within each religious community and human relations per se. We can notice that this is a great obstacle in proper integration of individuals and groups in a multicultural society like India that attempts to strive towards a nation. Hence, casteism appears to be no less an evil than communalism, and is equally a threat to national integration.

Some of the sinister fallouts of casteism for national integration are as follows.

One, if caste could be considered a component of social stratification within a religious community, then, it has the potential to put a hurdle in internal religious homogenisation, fragment the religious society with innumerable primordial divisions that get reflected in almost all walks of life, and produce micro-groups with differing and often conflictual interests and approaches within such a religious society. The scope of social interconnections and discourse gets narrower in that religious denomination, and members tend to judge issues not on its merits but on the basis of how they impact the interests of its smaller social splinters. The common holistic vision that is warranted for a well integrated religious society is relegated to the background and petty selfish micro-group interests take the front seats.

Two, casteism has the potential of breeding what Bhargava (2004) calls 'internal exclusions' that is quite detrimental to the well being of minorities within a religious community. The dalit Muslims in Islam and dalit Christians in Christianity are cases in point. This perpetuates injustice, intolerance and exclusion within a religious denomination. The most unfortunate part of this is that this gets subdued owing to the predominance of communal discourse in society with religious diversity. While multicultural societies may have learnt to exist in spite of such innumerable divisions, yet, it has been observed that usually neither the social nor the political leadership is able to integrate such intra-religious multitude into a kaleidoscopic social whole able to position itself vis-à-vis many other societies both at regional and global levels.

Three, casteism also prevents subaltern class formation. It keeps marginalised and downtrodden caste people so much preoccupied with their social identity that they are not able to connect to a common economic class across other social or religious groups either up or down the hierarchy.

Fourth, casteism, as communalism, perpetuates gender bias, subsumes gender into communal or caste trajectories, marginalises gender issues and prevents the formation of a women class. While communalism does it on the pretext of religious freedom, casteism does it on the basis of caste autonomy and by arguing that the upper caste/class women would dominate in any such gendered class, and women of weaker section coming from lower castes would be denied equal partnership in nation building and development. Thus, almost half the population is disallowed proper integration with society on one or the other pretext.

Given the Indian situation for the present, it is difficult to ignore the reality of communalism and casteism. They both torpedo social reforms within the communities and suppress struggles for economic reforms by dividing the poor on religious and casteist lines (EPW-Worsening Discrimination: 8 July, 1989, pp. 1489–1490). The fight against them may continue endlessly and may not yield quick dividends. But, can we allow ourselves to be dictated by these considerations, or will we formulate some proactive strategy to counter them effectively so that we can march towards the goal of national integration? Perhaps, there is a need to shift the discourse from national integration to inclusion and inclusive politics that may work as a foundation for social and national integration. The era of 'politics of identity and empowerment' must end and we must move to an era of 'people's welfare and national development' that may make everyone, irrespective of caste and religion, secure, contented and happy. That would make the issue of national integration more meaningful.

Shri Jawaharlal Nehru, our first Prime Minister, convened a National Integration Conference in September-October, 1961 to find ways and means to combat the evils of communalism, casteism, regionalism, linguism and narrow-mindedness, and to formulate definite conclusions in order to give a lead to the country. This Conference decided to set up a National Integration Council (NIC) to review all matters pertaining to national integration and make recommendations thereon.

Inaugurating the first National Integration Conference, the then Vice President Dr. S. Radhakrishnan said on 28 September 1961 that historically, India had always been a "multi-racial, multi-lingual, multi-religious society and there was never any question of saying that this group is the biggest or that is not the biggest. The idea was to accommodate all, and not to obliterate any faith but to harmonise all faiths. Even a very conservative legislator like Manu tells us that all the people should learn their own particular traditions...You find something similar in the Koran. There is said: 'O, Mankind, we created you from a single pair of a male and a female and made you into nations and tribes that you may know each other, not that you may despise each other'.' Such examples can also be cited fro other religious scriptures.

It is strange that in spite of the fact that most of our religions espouse the dictum of the oneness of God and the oneness of mankind, yet they fight for establishing the superiority of their own religion over that of others, their race over other races, their language over other languages and their caste or ethnicity over other castes or ethnicities. Any attempt to do so dents that oneness and harms that cohesiveness that comes from „individual consciousness connecting with the supreme consciousness through general consciousnesses.

National integration is basically a social bonding of love, respect and cooperation with fellow individuals of whatever religion, caste, language and region. Any primacy accorded to any of the primordial factors over that bonding is against national integration. Casteism and communalism both take us to creating differences between human beings. All differences are heading towards schisms; schisms are turning into hatred, hatred leading to active conflicts, active conflicts culminating into violence, and violence threatens social harmony, economic prosperity and national integration.

The present breed of leadership is so much short sighted that it focus on policies designed to divide people for political purposes and electoral gains. Instead of universalising the society and attempting for its socio-economic homogenisation through correct policies, we are stuck up at the affirmative action strategies for social justice in a mechanical way that caters to the vested interests of a certain caste category without allowing the real needy persons to be benefitted by those policies. That is breeding hatred and animosity within caste groups and between caste groups. Such developments cannot take us towards the goals of national integration. So, the need of the hour is to go far a radical revamping of our social justice policies and strategies that could diminish the feeling of exclusion among the marginalised and downtrodden sections of our society and push them towards inclusion that will be the only way to orient them towards national integration.

Note:

1. National Commission for Backward Classes. We can find state-wise Central List of OBCs- http://www.ncbc.nic.in/Centrallistifobc.html

REFERENCES

1. Ahmad Imtiaz (1973): 'Introduction', in Imtiaz Ahmad (ed.), Caste and Social Stratificaion among Muslims, Delhi, Manohar Book Service.
2. Ahmed Imtiaz (2009): 'Can there be a Category called Dalit Muslims?, Indian Dalit Muslim Voice, August 31. http://dalitmuslims.wordpress.com/2009/08/31/can-there-be-a-category-called-dalit-muslims/
3. Alam Anwar (2003): Democratisation of Indian Muslims. Economic and Political Weekly, XXXVIII (46) November 15.
4. Alam Javeed (1999): 'Is Caste Appeal Casteism? Oppressed Castes in Politics', Economic and Political Weekly, Vol. 34, No. 13 (March 27, April 2), pp. 757–761.
5. Ali Syed (2002): Collective and Elective Ethnicity: Caste among Urban Muslims in India, Sociological Forum, Vol. 17, No. 4, December, pp. 593–620.
6. Ansari Gaus (1959): Muslim Castes in Uttar Pradesh, Lucknow, Ethnographic and Folk Culture Society.

7. Anwar Ali (2001): Masawat ki Jung: Pasemanzar: Bihar ka Pasmanda Musalman (in Hindi). New Delhi. Vani Prakashan.
8. Bhargava Rajeev (2004): Inclusion and exclusion in South Asia: The Role of Religion, OCCASIONAL PAPER, Background paper for HDR 2004, United Nations Development Programme.
9. Bhowmik Sharit K. (1992): Caste and Class in India, Economic and Political Weekly, Vol. 27, No. 24/25 (Jun. 13–20), pp. 1246–1248.
10. Dorairaj S. (2011): 'Caste Divide', FRONTLINE, Volume 28 – Issue 04, Feb. 12–25, 2011.
11. Economic and Political Weekly (1989): Christian Dalits: Worsening Discrimination, Vol. 24, No. 27 (July 8), pp. 1489–90.
12. Economic and Political Weekly(1995): Dalit Christians: Victims of Injustice Vol. 30, No. 48 (Dec. 2), p. 3041.
13. Grewal J.S. (1972): 'Toynbee's Interpretation of Sikh History', From Guru Nank to Maharaja Ranjit Singh: Essays in Sikh History, Guru Nanak University, Amritsar.
14. Grewal J.S. (1994): The Sikhs of Punjab, The New Cambridge History of India, Indian Edition, Foundation Books, Delhi.
15. Hasnian Nadeem (2005): in H.S. Verma (ed.), The OBCs and the Ruling Classes in India, Jaipur, Rawat Publications, pp. 84–97.
16. Kader Salil, Social Stratification Among Muslims In India, 15 June, 2004, countercurrents.org from http://www.countercurrents.org/dalit-kader150604.htm
17. Krishnan P.S. (2010): Understanding the Backward Classes of Muslim Society, Economic and Political Weekly, Vol. 45, No. 34, 21–27 August, 2010.

18. Lindholm Charles (1965): 'Paradigms of Society: A Critique of Theories of Caste among Indian Muslims', European Journal of Sociology, pp. 131–140.

19. Namboodiripad E.M.S. (1979): 'Caste Conflicts vs Growing Unity of Popular Democratic Forces', Economic and Political Weekly, Vol. 14, No. 7/8, Annual Number: Class and Caste inIndia (February), pp. 329–331 + 333–336.

20. Puri Harish K. (2003): Scheduled Castes in Sikh Community: A Historical Perspective, Economic and Political Weekly, June 28, pp. 2693–2701.

21. Sahay Anand Mohan (2003, March 6): Backward Muslims protest denial of burial. News report in www.rediff.com. Retrieved on October 30 2003, from http://www.rediff.com/news/2003/mar/06bihar.htm

22. Sikand Yoginder (2003): The 'Dalit-Muslims' and the All India Backward Muslim Morcha. Qalandar, September. Retrieved November 12 2003, from http://www.islaminterfaith.org/sep2003/article.html

23. Singh Giani Pratap (1933): Jaat Paat ate Chhoot Chhaat Sabandhi Gurmat Sudhar (Punjabi), SGPC, Amritsar.

24. Srimanjari (1990): Seminar on 'Communalism in India': A Report, Social Scientist, Vol. 18, No. 6/7 (June-July), pp. 49–72.

6

Teacher Training at the UGC ASC, AMU: Towards Peace and Harmony in Society

S. Reshma Jamal

INTRODUCTION

India is a vast country, having a geographical area of 3287263 sq. kms. and a population of little more than one billion people. The subcontinent accommodated and integrated many communities and their ways of life from time to time. The human settlement in India had begun from early Stone Age and so far it has been the homeland of many communities who have contributed to its rich cultural heritage. However, narrow views about community, class, caste and region often result in fissiparous tendencies. To prevent the losses occurring to the society in terms of peace disruption and lack of solidarity to compete globally it has been the Government policy to promote national integration.

The UGC Academic Staff Colleges were established in 1987 in 47 Universities in India as part of National Policy on Education in order to orient the teaching staff towards the ideals of higher education in India. It includes issues and ethics relevant to socio-economic and educational development, being better teachers, being acquainted with modern technology and developing impressive personality traits. At the Aligarh Muslim University the ASC was founded in 1987 and the Orientation Programme (OP) for newly appointed lecturers of the universities and colleges has been regularly organized since then. As part of this programme the participants are sensitized with lectures by resource persons of specialized disciplines. The CPs also make teacher presentations and submit written assignments on various topics for evaluation- based grading.

Choosing from a list of many topics of relevance to education, culture and society the participants of the orientation programmes (OP) are imbued with the ideal of National Integration. They present their views on the subject and analyze its various aspects. The ideas and observations of these teacher candidates are presented in a term paper to be submitted as an assignment. This paper presents an account of the participant's perception on National Integration. A general estimation of the impact of this training and sensitization, as directed by the UGC, on the teachers of higher education in India is offered here.

METHODOLOGY

The term papers submitted by Orientation Programme participants of the last four years were analyzed. The level of enrichment on the issue was assessed by the language and content delivered. The data were collected on a scale of low and high on three categories vis-à-vis national integration:

A. The positive impact of National Integration and its necessity
B. The apple of discord in the society
C. Measures to maintain unity in cultural diversity

Participant's opinion expressed in the text of the assignment was analysed for its knowledge level on the following constructs under the categories mentioned above.

1. Positive Impact

(a) Peace and brotherhood beyond divisions are important for survival
(b) It is a matter of national pride that India is geographically and culturally diverse

(c) There is strength in solidarity to bear with foreign onslaughts
(d) The country can progress only when there is inclusive development for all

2. Causes of Discord

(a) Religion is the apple of discord in society
(b) Caste-based divisions in the society prevent people from national integration
(c) Languages and dialects of different types create divisions
(d) Culture varies from place to place and alienates people from one another

3. Means and Measures

(a) Media plays a proactive role in promoting national integration
(b) Government policies and programmes can integrate people
(c) Education goes a long way in ensuring that divisions in society are resolved
(d) Civil society is capable of maintaining social dialogue

Scores were assigned to each of the constructs above on the basis of the statements made and analysis was done using spreadsheets to calculate the respective strength of each construct. Owing to the pertinent aspect of national integration, the above-mentioned constructs are ranked according to the number of assignments giving them a high score. Percentage values are calculated and trends in the data are presented.

RESULTS

A total number of 15 Orientation Programmes were successfully conducted by the UGC ASC, AMU in the last four years i.e. 2006–07, 2007–08, 2008–09 and 2009–10. In these training programmes 539 participants were enrolled and they received certificates after completing all the components of the evaluation process. The written assignments on national integration were taken from each participant, hence for the purpose of this study 539 written assignments were analysed for their contents. Table 1 contains the break-up of these programmes over the last four academic sessions according to the strength of Course Participants (CPs).

S. No.	Year	No. of CPs
1.	2006-07 (OP- 96, 97, 98, 99)	85
2.	2007-08 (OP- 100, 101, 102, 103)	130
3.	2009-10 (OP- 104, 105, 106)	97
4.	2010-11 (OP- 107,108,109,110)	127

Table 1: Participants, sensitization regarding the positive effects of national integration and its needs sensitization for India

S. No.	Factor	No. of CPs giving High Score	Value (%)
1.	Peace and brotherhood beyond divisions are important for survival	**130**	**24**
2.	It is a matter of national pride that India is geographically and culturally diverse	**109**	**20**
3.	There is strength in solidarity to bear with foreign onslaughts	**100**	**19**
4.	The country can progress only when there is inclusive development for all	**200**	**37**
TOTAL			100

Table 2: Level of education regarding the factors which divide the society

S. No.	Factor	No. of CPs giving High Score	Value (%)
1.	Religion is the apple of discord regarding national integration	197	37
2.	Caste-based divisions in the society prevent people from national integration	203	38
3.	Languages and dialects of different types create divisions	80	17
4.	Culture varies from place to place and secludes people from one another	50	10
TOTAL			100

Table 3: Opinion regarding the factors which play a proactive role in promoting and ensuring national integration

S. No.	Factor	No. of CPs giving High Score	Value (%)
1.	Media plays a proactive role in promoting national integration	109	20
2.	Government policies and programmes can integrate people	219	40
3.	Education goes a long way in ensuring that divisions in society are resolved	111	21
4.	Civil society is capable of maintaining social dialogue	100	19
TOTAL			100

DISCUSSION

Indian society in ancient, medieval and modern times always exhibited an underlying unity that created a composite culture, which is decisively pan-Indian in nature. Based on the generous conception Vasudhaiva Kutumbkam (the world is one family), we have a great cultural heritage. The innate unity of India is harmonized in its National Anthem – *"Punjab, Sindhu, Gujrat, Maratha,/Dravida, Utkala Benga..."* India's unity had been both politico-geographic and cultural in nature. The diversities have remained, but simultaneously provided a mainstream culture. Indian culture is dynamic, varied and tolerant. Though the foreign cultures retained their basic character, they became a part of the Indian culture with the passage of time. The diversity contributes to the variety and richness of Indian culture and strengthens national unity. Through all these diversities and differences there runs the invisible link of common culture, common civility, common heritage, the same form of greeting one another, the same form of respect shown to elders. There are the Vedas, the Bhagwad Gita, the Ramayana and the Mahabharata, the festivals, national symbols and finally the struggle for Independence that united the whole of Indian people.

The Aryans, Dravidians, Saka, Huns, Mongols and Europeans have all theoretically, created a society that is diverse. But actually, seldom has there been a social group, which has not merged into the mainstream of Indian national culture. Hospitality and charity are the hallmarks of Indian social tradition. Napoleon described India as "the birth-place of all metaphysics" alluding to its philosophical unity.

Divisive forces rear their ugly heads in the form of communalism, regionalism and casteism. The most unfortunate fact is that the legacy of British rule still persists. Communal riots still break out owing to many factors. There is still a feeling of veiled hostility between the two communities. The British had encouraged communalism because a division between Hindus and Muslims made it easier for them to control our country. Unfortunately, even after the passage of time these communal feelings have not ended. More than fifty years after Independence communal feelings still exist 'One of the great barriers to integration in India has been the highly unfavorable images the two major religious communities of India have of each other'. (Gani, H.A: 1978)

Regionalism is another barrier to national integration. The adaptation of federation with unitary characteristics by the Indian constitution is an excellent device to reconcile national unity with regional diversity. National unity is not affected by one's genuine love for his native place, its language and culture, but it is impeded when regional loyalty and regional interests based on parochialism are advocated. While at the national level India is a federal society in which language groups and religious minorities have an important role, each state is a plural society in which castes and communal groups play a political role (Nayar: 1966).

It is not only unfortunate but alarming to note that casteism in India has a strong foothold. Although universal adult franchise has been there in India, it has not done away with caste consciousness, rather accentuated it. Politicians thrive on capitalizing on the malady of casteism. Candidates are proposed and elected on the basis of caste.

Language is undoubtedly another sensitive issue in the context of national integration. The three language formula is a practical solution to the problem, but it is a temporary one. National integration is essential for social peace and harmony too. The safety and prosperity of our country depends upon our unity. Our states are like parts of our body. Prosperity of different states means the progress of the whole country.

Extremism is the act of spreading fear by threatening the people through illegal means to gain selfish interests. It ignores human values. Unemployment, lack of proper education and inadequate means of livelihood, lead to extremism. National integration fosters nationalism. It is opposed to communalism, linguistic jingoism, regionalism and other divisive tendencies.

According to the Indian Education Commission Report (1964–66) social and national integration is the major problem which will have to be tackled on several fronts, including education. Education can and should play a very significant role in it by

1. Introducing a common school system of public education
2. Making social and national service an integral part of education at all stages.
3. Promoting national consciousness.

In fact the teacher is the pivot in the organization of all programmes of national importance. Students are inspired by his views. The teacher directly impacts on the minds of children. All this depends on the personal philosophy of the teacher. So it is essential that the teacher should himself be a model. His own view should not be narrow and should not have a pessimistic approach to the national issues. National consciousness should be visible in the conduct of teachers and they should themselves employ a national approach while teaching the subject.

The media has symbiotic relationship with democracy. Media can perform various functions in promoting National Integration. Broadly speaking, media can help contribute in three spheres of activity – Economic, Sociological and Political. In the sphere of economic inputs media can help people find alternative ways of making a living which will reduce the pressure on land and raise a family's economic status. Media can help create, demand for goods and motivate local initiative to meet rising demands.

In the sociological sphere of activity media aids the process of status change from heredity to achievement. To do this, it his successfully motivated the illiterate to become literate in our society. Media can help shift influence from age and traditional status to knowledge and ability and thus reduce the sharp caste and class differences in the society. It should spread the message of love and brotherhood.

In the political sphere of its activity media helps in the process, of power change from heredity to achievement. It motivates traditional leaders to defend their power by raising their information level and helps the masses recognize their own importance in the power structure and act as a stimulus to political participation.

CONCLUSION

The UGC Academic Staff College, AMU has been successfully fulfilling its duty of promoting the cause of healthy society and unity in diverse cultures of India by sensitizing the course participants of the Orientation Programme through its lectures, teacher presentations and written assignments regarding the values of national integration. They understand the role of teachers and education in promoting oneness of the Indian people but also recognize the need to complement it with existing democratic institutions of the government and media. It is also felt that the discords of society found in religious sectarianism, linguistic identities and the morass of casteism should be tackled in the classroom by broad-minded teachers. Moreover, the time spent by the Course Participants in the Orientation Programmes gives them an excellent opportunity to interact with one another and form a group cohesion beyond identities. The residential participants have a better opportunity to live together and reach out to the various cultures of the country. This develops a person-to-person contact and goes a long way in dissuading identity based prejudices, if any, at the pan-India level.

Thus, national integration means a feeling of oneness among all Indians. All our countrymen must feel emotionally integrated. We must think that we are Indians first and members of a particular religion, region or caste afterwards. This can be achieved when we teach the same to our children. All the children, during their formative years, must be taught that we all are Indians belonging to the one motherland. We must not believe in separate identities. It is time to merge in one mainstream. Unless we develop a sense of unity and give up our narrow outlook, we might not be able to survive for long as a nation. It is unity in spite of great differences. In other words, unity in diversity. The most important factor is the fundamental unity of India about which volumes have been written (Mookerji: 1970).

India today is a unified, strong and vibrant nation. It is evoking an 'intense belief' in its future in the minds of many like Nandan Nilekani, who writes, "I still think that after a long and convoluted path, after many a stumble and wrong turn, a different kind of moment seems to be upon us. For the first time, there is a sense of hope across the country, which I believe is universal. There is a momentum for change, evident in the enthusiasm of our younger legislators, the mushrooming of civil society organizations, and activists fighting in the courts for reforms in Governance and for the protection of fundamental rights."

REFERENCES

Gani, H.A. (1978): *Muslim Political Issues and National Integration*, New Delhi: Sterling Publishers.

Mookerji, Radha Kumud (1970): *Fundamental Unity of India*, Bharatiya Vidya Bhavan, Bombay.

Nilekani, Nandan (2008): *Imaging India: Ideas for the New Century*, Penguin, New Delhi.

Sukumsran Nayar, V.K. (1966): "*New challenges Before Indian Federalism*", Kerala Journal of Political Studies, 1.1.

Olive Peacock (1991): *Minorities and National Integration in India, Arihant Publishers, Jaipur.*

HINDI

1

भारत-विभिन्न संस्कृतियों का केन्द्र

डॉ. रीता बागची

हमारे देश भारत में जीवन के हर विभाग में विभिन्नता पाई जाती है, यहाँ कई सभ्यताएँ एवं संस्कृतियाँ मौजूद हैं। बहुत सी भाषाएँ एवं बोलियाँ बोली जाती हैं। विभिन्न धर्मों के मानने वाले रहते हैं, न जाने कितनी जातियाँ, कबीले और नसली गिरोह अपने विशेष रीति-रिवाज, रहन-सहन, साहित्य एवं संगीत के कारण अपनी अलग पहचान रखते हैं। इस महान देश में अनेकता की यह अधिकता देश की अखण्डता के लिये एक अनमोल उपहार है, जिसने इसका नाम विश्व में ऊँचा कर रखा है। समाज में तरह-तरह की संस्कृतियों की बहार अति सुंदर एवं अमूल्य है। भारत के प्राचीन इतिहास एवं सभ्यताओं के उभरने एवं प्रगति करने की कहानी अति रोचक एवं उपदेश देने वाली है जो हमको याद दिलाती है कि अत्यधिक विरोधों के उपरांत भी यह देश सदैव एक रहा है और विभिन्न राज्य अपनी-अपनी पहचान के साथ अनेक सभ्यताओं को देश की एकता के परिदृश्य में प्रस्तुत कर रहे हैं। निःसंदेह कभी-कभी इन विरोधों के कारण लड़ाई या खींचातानी की शक्ल उत्पन्न हो जाती है। हमारे महान नेता पं. जवाहर लाल नेहरू के अनुसार ''हमारे देश एवं राष्ट्र की एकता कहीं बाहर से नहीं आयी, अपितु यह आपसी मेलमिलाप की प्राचीन परंपरा, जिसे यहाँ के लोगों ने अपनी खुशी और इच्छा से स्वीकार किया है; पर निर्भर है।''

यह सत्य है कि भारतीय संघ, विभिन्न सभ्यताओं और पहचान का एक संयुक्त प्लेटफार्म है जहाँ हिमालय से लेकर कन्याकुमारी और पंजाब से लेकर दिल्ली एवं पूर्वी क्षेत्रों तक धर्म, भाषा, रीतिरिवाज, रहन-सहन के नमूने समाज के आर्थिक, सामाजिक एवं सांस्कृतिक घेरों में जीते-जागते और जगमगाते दिखाई देते हैं। संयुक्त राष्ट्र के इस धारे ने धर्मनिरपेक्ष शासन, सामाजिक न्याय, आपसी मेलमिलाप और मानवीयता को जन्म दिया और परवान चढ़ाया। यह कोई मामूली कार्य नहीं है।

हमें गर्व है कि हमारे देश में एक से अधिक संस्कृतियाँ, धर्म और भाषाएँ हैं जिनको राष्ट्रीय स्तर पर माना जाता है और उनका आदर किया जाता है। इस कारण मानवता एवं मानवीय मूल्यों को बड़ा लाभ हुआ है। पक्षपात, एक दूसरे में अंतर करना, घृणा की भावनाओं और उनके कारणों को रोकने में हमारे देश के सांस्कृतिक एवं सामाजिक विरोधाभास ने बड़ी सहायता की है और इससे एक दूसरे को समझना अत्यधिक सरल हो गया है।

आज हमको लोगों, विभिन्न आर्थिक, सामाजिक एवं सांस्कृतिक समूहों की पहचान, उनको मानने और उनके साथ काम करने में कोई कठिनाई नहीं होती। आपसी मेलमिलाप और दोस्ती का यह सिलसिला देश में दूर-दूर तक पाया जाता है। इससे बढ़कर खुशी और संतोष की क्या बात हो सकती है। भारतीय जनता की विभिन्न विशेषताओं में हमारे देश की पहचान को दृढ़ बनाया है और हर एक के हृदय में बसाया है।

हमारे देश की सभ्यता की धरोहर हज़ारों वर्ष पुरानी है। विश्व के विभिन्न लोगों की सभ्यता, धर्म, भाषा एवं रीति-रिवाजों ने हमारे देश की सांस्कृतिक एवं सामाजिक प्रगति पर बड़ा असर डाला है। जो अच्छा भी है और बुरा भी। यहाँ के पुराने रहने वाले द्रविड़ों ने हिन्दू सभ्यता एवं संस्कृति की नींव डाली जिसको आर्यों ने विभिन्न दृष्टिकोणों और स्वस्थ परंपराओं से संवारा और सजाया है। वैदिक सभ्यता, सिंधु घाटी की सभ्यता और उसके बाद शक, हूण, कुश, बुद्ध, जैन, यूनानियों, मुसलमानों और ईसाइयों से मेलजोल और उनके प्रभाव से भारत की संयुक्त संस्कृति उत्पन्न हुई जो आज तक पूरे आब व ताब के साथ मौजूद है। इतिहास हमें यह बताता है कि प्रारंभ में हिन्दू वैदिक धर्म बड़ा सीधा-साधा था। धीरे-धीरे उसमें नई चीज़ें जोड़ी गयीं, कुछ खराबियाँ भी पैदा हुईं जिसका लोगों ने विरोध भी किया। बुद्ध, जैन और सिख धर्म पैदा हुए। नये-नये संप्रदाय और संस्थाओं का जन्म हुआ किन्तु देश की केंद्रीयता बनी रही। जाति, पाति, हिन्दू दर्शन, भक्ति आंदोलन और हिन्दुमत पर दूसरे सामी धर्मों के प्रभाव ने भी भारत की संयुक्त संस्कृति को बहुत कुछ दिया।

भारत में धर्मों की अधिकता ने भी महत्त्वपूर्ण प्रभाव डाले हैं। उन्होंने भारत के सामाजिक एवं सांस्कृतिक जीवन के प्रारंभिक नियमों के बनाने में सहायता की है। इस सिलसिले में दुनिया के आठ बड़े धर्मों में हिन्दू धर्म, इस्लाम, ईसाईयत, सिखमत, बुद्ध मत, जैन मत, यहूदियत और जरतुश्ती (पारसी) के नाम हमारे

सामने आते हैं। जिनके विश्वास, नियम, पूजा करने का तरीका, सच्चाई, सदाचार और रहन-सहन के तौर तरीके एक दूसरे से भिन्न होने के बावजूद आपस में कुछ मिली जुली बातें भी होती हैं। और एक दूसरे की पहचान आदर और सम्मान के साथ करते हैं। इस संबंध में हिन्दुओं के भक्ति आंदोलन, इस्लाम में सूफ़ियों की परंपरा और गुरू नानक के नियमों ने सामूहिक जीवन और सामाजिक मेल मिलाप, सदाचार और अच्छे संबंध पैदा करने में विशेष भाग लिया। भारत में धर्म के अंतर्गत लगभग संपूर्ण जीवन होता है और प्रत्येक धर्मों के मानने वाले बराबरी और विश्वास की स्वतंत्रता के अधिकारों के मालिक होते हैं। उनका अपना पूज्य स्थान या पूजा के तरीके, रहने-सहने के तरीके और नियम-क़ानून और अपनी संस्थाएँ होती हैं। जिनके द्वारा वह अपने धर्म और सामाजिक व धार्मिक मूल्यों की सुरक्षा और उन्हें आगे बढ़ाने का काम करते हैं। भारत के संविधान ने समान अधिकारों के आधार पर उनकी पूरी सुरक्षा की ज़मानत दी है और सब धर्मों को समानता का स्थान दिया है।

भारत में इस्लाम के आने से सभ्यता एवं संस्कृति और सामाजिक जीवन पर बड़ा अधिक प्रभाव पड़ा है क्योंकि इस्लाम के एक बड़े धर्म होने के कारण विभिन्न नसलों, रंगों और विरोधी विशेषताएँ रखने वाले लोगों ने इसे स्वीकार किया। उदाहरणार्थ अरबी, ईरानी, अफगानी, अफरीकी, योरोपियन, एशियाई इत्यादि। यह समझना उचित नहीं कि मुसलमानों के आने से पूर्व भारत में केवल हिन्दू ही रहते थे। भारत का प्राचीन इतिहास बताता है कि अशोक बुद्धमत को मानने वाला था और देश के विभिन्न भागों में बौद्ध मठ मौजूद थे। इस्लाम से पूर्व ईसाई, पारसी और यहूदी भारत आ चुके थे किन्तु यह बात भी ठीक है कि इस्लाम के मुकाबले में किसी धर्म ने इतना गहरा प्रभाव नहीं छोड़ा। मुसलमान सदियों से अपने हिन्दू देश वासियों के साथ मिलजुल कर रह रहे हैं। मुग़लों ने अपने वतन को भुला कर हिन्दुस्तान में अपना विशाल शासन स्थापित किया और यहाँ के जीवन में खूब घुल मिल गए। भारत की संस्कृति में जो उनका योगदान है उसे कभी भुलाया नहीं जा सकता। हिन्दुस्तान में मुस्लिम शासकों और इस्लाम ने अत्यधिक प्रभाव डाला है। जनसंख्या के बड़े हिस्से ने ऊँच-नीच और सामाजिक बुराईयों से तंग आकर इस्लाम धर्म स्वीकार कर लिया। बराबरी, न्याय और अधिकारों की पूर्ति ने इस्लाम को ख़ूब फैलाया। मुसलमान सरदारों, व्यापारियों, शिल्पकारों और फौजियों ने यहाँ के पिछड़े और कमजोर वर्ग के

लोगों की सामाजिक आर्थिक, आध्यात्मिक और शैक्षिक उन्नति प्राप्त करने में हर प्रकार की सहायता की। मुग़ल शासन काल में साहित्य, निर्माण, संगीत और दूसरी शिल्प कलाओं की उन्नति के साथ, आर्थिक संपन्नता, बराबरी और सदाचार की अधिकता ने बड़ा अच्छा प्रभाव डाला। स्वामी विवेकानंद ने भारत के इसलामी काल को सभ्यता व संस्कृति एवं उन्नति का सुनहरा दौर बताया है। इसी प्रकार प्रसिद्ध इतिहासकार ताराचंद और प्रो. आर.सी. मजूमदार ने रीतिरिवाज, खानपान, पहनावा, रहनसहन, साहित्य और विभिन्न ज्ञान-विज्ञान में मुसलमानों की बुनियादी भूमिका का वर्णन प्रशंसनात्मक ढंग से किया है। स्वयं मुसलमानों ने क्षेत्रीय प्रभाव, अपने रहन-सहन और जीवन के दूसरे भागों में स्वीकार किये जिसके कारण संयुक्त या गंगा जमुनी संस्कृति उत्पन्न हुई। ताजमहल एवं दूसरी ऐतिहासिक इमारतों में इस्लामी प्रभाव के साथ हिन्दू, बुद्ध, जैन और ईरानी विशेषताओं की झलक भी दिखाई देती है। इस मिली जुली भारत की संस्कृति में विभिन्न इलाकों के रीतिरिवाज, भाषा, धर्म इत्यादि की नुमाइंदगी भी मिलती है जो हर प्रकार से प्रशंसनीय है। सभ्यता एवं संस्कृति बलपूर्वक किसी पर थोपी नहीं जा सकती। यही कारण है कि इतना समय बीत जाने के बाद भी देश के चप्पे-चप्पे में विरोध में मेल मिलाप और राष्ट्रीय एकता के नमूने मिलते हैं। आमतौर पर क्षेत्रीयता के देव को अलगाववाद और अकेन्द्रियता के साथ जोड़ा जाता है किन्तु भारत के इतिहास और परंपरा ने इस प्रभाव को ग़लत साबित किया है। यहाँ विभिन्न क्षेत्रों और राज्यों ने अपने शैक्षिक एवं आर्थिक पिछड़ेपन के विरुद्ध आवाज़ उठाई और आंदोलन किये। हमारे संविधान और शासन ने उन पर ध्यान दिया और उनकी शिकायतों को सहानुभूति पूर्वक दूर करने के प्रयत्न भी किये। मेल मिलाप और न्याय की माँग भी यही है कि राष्ट्रीयता के लाभ के लिये देश के सभी इलाकों को शिक्षा, आर्थिक एवं सामाजिक उन्नति के अवसर बराबरी के साथ प्रदान किये जायें।

भाषा और बोलियों की समस्या

भाषा सबकी समझ में आने वाला एक ऐसा साधन है जिससे हम शिक्षा, दर्शन, इतिहास, सभ्यता एवं संस्कृति, समाज एवं अर्थ व्यवस्था बल्कि जीवन के हर पहलू से संबंधित जानकारी हासिल कर सकते हैं और दूसरों तक पहुँचा सकते

हैं। हमारे देश में तीन सौ पच्चीस भाषायँ और पच्चीस लिपियाँ मौजूद है जिनमें से अट्ठारह भाषाओं को संविधान ने राष्ट्रीय भाषाओं का स्थान दिया है और बाक़ी को क्षेत्रीय भाषा बताया है जिनके द्वारा शिक्षा, मातृ भाषा में आसानी से दी जा सकती है। हमारे देश की सरकारी भाषा हिन्दी के साथ अंग्रेज़ी भी है मगर हिन्दी के कट्टर मानने वाले देश प्रेम के नाम पर चाहते हैं कि केवल हिन्दी, देवनागरी लिपि के साथ सरकारी भाषा बनाई जाय। यह बात दूसरी भाषाओं वाले राज्यों के नागरिकों को पसंद नहीं, और न्याय से मेल नहीं खाती। बुद्धि एवं न्याय की बात यह है कि हिन्दी, अंग्रेज़ी और क्षेत्रीय भाषाओं के सहयोग से काम चलाना चाहिए और इसी प्रकार देश में अनुशासन, शिक्षा और एक दूसरे को समझने का सही और असरदार प्रबंध किया जा सकता है।

जातिपांति और क़बीलों की समस्या

हमारे देश के सामाकि ढांचे में जातिपांति और गोत्र विशेष स्थान रखते हैं जिनका सीधा संबंध विवाह, व्यवसाय और रहनसहन से है। इसकी बड़ी खराबियाँ छूतछात, जन्म के आधार पर शोषण और ऊँची जाति वालों का निचली जातियों से अमानवीय एवं क्रूरतापूर्ण व्यवहार हैं जो सदियों से चले आ रहे हैं। इन परिस्थितियों को बदलने की शीघ्र आवश्यकता है। ऊँची जाति वालों को अपना ग़लत रास्ता बदलना चाहिए और देश चलाने वालों का कर्त्तव्य है कि वह निचली जाति वालों की खराब शैक्षिक एवं आर्थिक दशा को ठीक करें और उनको बराबरी के अधिकार दें।

इसी के साथ आदिवासी लोगों की समस्या भी महत्त्वपूर्ण है जो मूल राष्ट्रीय धारे से अलग हैं। अपने विशेष रीति-रिवाज और अलग भावनाएँ रखते हैं। वह गरीबी, अशिक्षा और कुछ सामाजिक बुराईयों के शिकार हैं। हमारा कर्त्तव्य है कि उनके सुधार के लिये आवश्यक प्रयास करें। उनकी आदिवासी धरोहर और परंपराओं की सुरक्षा के साथ उनको पूरा अवसर दिया जाये कि वह हर प्रकार की उन्नति कर के राष्ट्रीय धारा में अपनी जगह बना सकें। अंग्रेज़ों के चले जाने के बाद भारत स्वतंत्र प्रजातंत्र बन गया है। इसका उत्तरदायित्व है कि देश के अल्पसंख्यक एवं पिछड़े वर्गों की भलाई के लिये विशेष योजनाएँ बनाएँ। हमारे संविधान में इसकी पूरी गुंजाइश है कि देश के विभिन्न वर्गों की भाषा, धर्म,

रीति-रिवाज और सांस्कृतिक विशेषताओं की सुरक्षा की जाये और उनको राष्ट्रीय धरोहर और संयुक्त संस्कृति में आदर एवं सम्मान के साथ जगह दी जाये।

आज चारों ओर मानव अधिकार और मूल्यों की सुरक्षा की माँग हो रही है। भारत में भी यह समस्या बड़ी महत्त्वपूर्ण है। देश का फेडरल और केन्द्रीय चरित्र इस बात की मांग करता है कि राजनीतिक रूप से तो देश एकताबद्ध रहे किन्तु सभ्यता एवं संस्कृति के स्तर पर अलग रहने की सबको आज़ादी हो। राज्य का कर्त्तव्य है कि वह एकता में अनेकता के नियम पर कटिबद्ध रहे।

दुख की बात है कि हमारे देश में इस बारे में कहने और करने में खासा अंतर पाया जाता है। अवसरवादिता, बेईमानी, स्वार्थ, जातपात का कट्टरपन और दूसरे ग़लत कार्यों के कारण राष्ट्रीय एकता और हमारी संयुक्त संस्कृति को खतरा हो रहा है। धर्म और भाषा के पक्षपात एवं कट्टरपन ने धर्म और भाषाओं की अधिकता के लाभ को धुंधला दिया है। इस उपद्रव को कुचलने की कड़ी आवश्यकता है। हालात नाजुक और ख़राब अवश्य हैं मगर निराशा की बात नहीं। अंधकार के वातावरण में आशा की किरण मौजूद है अर्थात उचित सुधार के प्रयत्न करने से इस प्रकार की उलझनों को दूर किया जा सकता है जिसका दायित्व इस देश के सभी नागरिकों पर है।

2

राष्ट्रीय एकीकरण – भारत का सफल अनुभव

प्रो. मिर्ज़ा अस्मर बेग

समाज शास्त्र के विद्वान लेखकों, जिनमें मैक्स-वेबर से लेकर पीटर बर्गर तक सम्मिलित हैं, उनका विचार है कि एकीकरण अथवा अधार्मिकता वर्तमान समय का एक मजबूत और रुचिकर उपहार है जो एक ही समय में नागरिक जीवन की सुविधाओं, बौद्धिक विकास, अल्पसंख्यकों, व्यवसायिक कुशलता, स्फूर्तिदायक प्रबंधन का संग्रह है जिसमें किसी भी धार्मिक विश्वास या रीति-रिवाज को समाप्त करने का कोई स्थान नहीं होता। अधार्मिकता की कल्पना विश्व में सन् 1648 में जन्मी, जब मसीही कलीसा का अधिकार एवं सत्ता राजाओं की तरफ़ हस्तांतरित हो गई और फ्रांस, इग्लैंड और पाश्चात्य देशों में धार्मिक संबंधों में राष्ट्र को निर्णय लेने का अधिकार दिया गया और एकीकरण की सोच को उन्नति का प्रतीक बताया गया। यहाँ यह बात स्पष्ट करना आवश्यक है कि एकीकरण शब्द का अर्थ और व्याख्या विभिन्न देशों में पाये जाने वाले ऐतिहासिक एवं सांस्कृतिक माहौल के अनुसार अलग-अलग स्पष्ट किये गये हैं। जैसे अमेरिका और भारत में इसका अर्थ एक दूसरे से बिल्कुल भिन्न है। भारत में एकीकरण का अर्थ यह है कि राष्ट्र अथवा सत्ता किसी धर्म की विरोधी अथवा मानने वाली नहीं, और उसके अधर्मी होने का सबसे बड़ा प्रमाण यह है कि यहाँ हर धर्म के अनुयाइयों को धार्मिक स्वतंत्रता एवं समानता प्रदान की गई है। पश्चिमी देशों में यह शब्द धर्म के प्रतिकूल अर्थ रखता है अर्थात् एकीकरण से तात्पर्य धर्म के प्रतिकूल रुझान लिया जाता है। और इसकी नींव उन ऐतिहासिक घटनाओं पर है जिनके कारण चर्च और शासकों में संघर्ष की दशा उत्पन्न हो गई और शासकों ने चर्च और धार्मिक संस्थाओं को सामाजिक उत्थान और अधिकार से वंचित कर दिया, इसके विरुद्ध संगठित और नकारात्मक बर्ताव पर जोर दिया। इसका उत्तरदायित्व धार्मिक परिधि की संकुचित एवं कठोर नीति पर भी है।

किन्तु सौभाग्य वश भारत में ऐसा नहीं हुआ। यहाँ के संविधान में स्पष्ट रूप से यह घोषित कर दिया गया कि प्रजातांत्रिक भारत का कोई सरकारी धर्म नहीं है और वह हर धर्म के साथ न्याय एवं समानता का व्यवहार करेगा। इस देश के देशवासियों को धर्म, विश्वास एवं आस्था की पूरी स्वतंत्रता होगी। इसलिए इसे याद रखना आवश्यक है कि भारत में एकीकरण का विचार आया तो पश्चिम से है किन्तु इसका अर्थ वहाँ से बिल्कुल भिन्न है। अब अमेरिका के संविधान के प्रथम संशोधन को देखिए जिस में कहा गया है कि "अमेरिकी की कांग्रेस (पार्लियामेन्ट) किसी धर्म के निर्माण अथवा उसको स्वीकार करने के विरुद्ध कोई क़ानून नहीं बनायेगी।" अमरीकी राष्ट्रपति जेफरसन ने इसकी व्याख्या करते हुए कहा था कि हमारे संविधान ने चर्च और राष्ट्र के बीच एक स्पष्ट रेखा बना दी है। इसी तरह की बातें आस्ट्रेलिया के संविधान में भी कही गई है कि धर्म के अनुकूल अथवा प्रतिकूल ना तो कोई क़ानून बनाया जायेगा और न किसी प्रकार का धार्मिक पैमाना अथवा परीक्षा आम सेवाओं के लिये रखी जायेगी।

भारतीय एकीकरण का अर्थ एवं उसकी विशेषताएँ

भारतीय संविधान, जो 26 जनवरी सन् 1950 को हमारे देश में लागू हुआ इसमें एकीकरण की व्याख्या इस प्रकार की गई है।

1. राष्ट्र या राज्य का कोई धर्म नहीं होगा।
2. सरकारी आय को किसी धर्म की उन्नति के लिये प्रयोग नहीं किया जायेगा।
3. सत्ता के लिये आवश्यक होगा कि धारा 25 के तहत दी गयी धार्मिक स्वतंत्रता के अधिकारों से संबंधित और आर्थिक या सांस्कृतिक कार्यों के प्रति अधार्मिक बर्ताव अपनाये और इस पर ध्यान दे।
4. छुआ-छूत को संविधान के अनुसार अवैधानिक और एक अपराध घोषित किया गया है। (धारा-17)
5. संविधान की धारा 25 के अंतर्गत हर नागरिक को यह अधिकार होगा कि वह जिस धर्म अथवा आस्था को चाहे ग्रहण करे किन्तु शासनव्यवस्था, सद्व्यवहार और जनता के स्वास्थ्य को ध्यान में रखते हुए इन अधिकारों

पर सत्ता कानूनी प्रतिबंध लगा सकती है। इसी के साथ यह अधिकार संविधान में लागू किये गये मूल अधिकार के अंतर्गत होंगे।

6. देश की अदालतें विशेषकर सुप्रीम कोर्ट, इस बारे में संविधान की व्याख्याओं के अनुसार सत्ता के आदेशों की जाँच पड़ताल करती रहेगी। सन् 1973 में केशव नन्द भारती के विरुद्ध केरल राज्य के मुकद्दमे में सुप्रीम कोर्ट ने अपने निर्णय में यह बात साफ की कि भारतीय संविधान के अनुसार एकीकरण एक आधारभूत एवं महत्वपूर्ण भाग है और इसके समर्थन में सन् 1975 में इन्दिरा गांधी और राज नारायण के मध्य चल रहे मुकद्दमे में सुप्रीम कोर्ट ने अपना एक और निर्णय सुनाया।

किन्तु हमारे देश में राष्ट्र और धार्मिक संस्थाओं के मध्य कोई भी विरोध नहीं पाया जाता। हमारे संविधान की धारा 16(5) में धार्मिक संस्थाओं के प्रबंध के लिये नियम बनाने की अनुमति नागरिकों को देती है। इसी प्रकार आस्था एवं धार्मिक अधिकारों की स्वतंत्रता धारा 25 और 26 के अंतर्गत हर नागरिक को दी गई है। निःसंदेह सत्ता के प्रबंधन, सद्व्यवहार और जनस्वास्थ्य के लिए एवं मौलिक अधिकारों की सुरक्षा के लिए उन पर कानूनी प्रतिबंध लगाने का अधिकार होगा जिसकी जाँच देश की अदालतें विशेष रूप से सुप्रीम कोर्ट करती रहेगी। अतः कोई भी भारतवासी नागरिक अथवा संस्था धार्मिक अथवा जनहित संबंधी संस्थाएँ स्थापित कर सकता है और देश के कानून के अंतर्गत उसके लिए चल या अचल सम्पत्ति का क्रय-विक्रय कर सकता है और उनकी व्यवस्था कर सकता है। इसमें शैक्षिक संस्थाएँ भी सम्मिलित हैं और इस सुविधा का द्वार केवल अल्पसंख्यकों के लिये नहीं बल्कि समाज के हर वर्ग एवं संप्रदाय द्वारा निर्मित शैक्षिक संस्थाओं के लिए खुला हुआ है।

अगर शैक्षिक संस्थाओं में धर्म से संबंधित शिक्षा दी जाती है तो हमारा संविधान इसे एकीकरण के विरुद्ध नहीं मानता है। इसका कहना यह है कि बिना पहचान खोये हमारे देश में सभी धर्मों की शिक्षा दी जा सकती है। शर्त यह है कि देश की क़ानून व्यवस्था के अंतर्गत हो।

इस तरह राज्य, सरकारी आय (जिसका अधिकांश भाग करों के रूप में नागरिकों से प्राप्त होता है।) का कुछ हिस्सा धार्मिक संस्थाओं अथवा धार्मिक

उत्सवों के लिये धारा 27 के तहत दे सकती है। जैसे-तमिलनाडु और केरला की राज्य सरकारें कुछ हिन्दू मन्दिरों की सहायता के लिये धन देती हैं जिनको स्वतंत्रता से पूर्व भारत के राजा सहायता दिया करते थे। जबकि अमेरिका के सुप्रीम कोर्ट ने एक निर्णय में यह कहा कि बच्चों को रोमन कैथोलिक स्कूल तक जाने का खर्च देने का अधिकार राज्य का नहीं है। हाँ यह बात अवश्य है कि सरकारी शैक्षिक संस्थाओं में जिनका सारा खर्च सत्ता सहन करती है किसी धर्म की शिक्षा 28(ए) के अन्तर्गत नहीं दी जा सकती, किन्तु जो संस्थाएँ किसी ट्रस्ट, वक़्फ बोर्ड अथवा नागरिकों ने स्थापित की हैं और वहाँ किसी विशेष धर्म की शिक्षा दी जाती है तो इनको सरकार आर्थिक सहायता दे सकती है और उनके अस्तित्व को स्वीकार कर सकती है।

इन बातों से स्पष्ट होता है कि भारतीय संविधान, अमेरिका के संविधान की तरह धार्मिक संस्थाओं से सत्ता का बिल्कुल असंबंधित रहना अथवा इनसे बिल्कुल अलग रहना पसंद नहीं करता। अपितु वह सत्ता को प्रेरणा देता है कि उचित अधार्मिकता के अन्तंगत वो सभी धर्मों से बराबरी का बर्ताव करें।

भारत में एकीकरण का प्रयोग सफल रहा है और इससे राष्ट्रीय एकता और भाईचारे को बड़ी शक्ति प्राप्त हुई है। किन्तु इसी के साथ यह भी सत्य है कि कुछ राजनीतिक, धार्मिक चिंतक और इससे भी अधिक रुचिकर बात यह है कि कुछ कट्टरपंथी धार्मिक वर्गों और स्वतंत्र विचार वाले वर्गों, दोनों की ओर से एकीकरण का विरोध यह कहकर किया जा रहा है कि वह नवीनीकरण एवं उन्नति के रास्ते में बाधा बन रहा है। इसी तरह एक प्रकार का सांस्कृतिक युद्ध एकीकरण के समर्थकों और विरोधियों के मध्य हो रहा है जिसमें बुद्धिजीवी, पत्रकार, धार्मिक विद्वान, अदालतें और मीडिया सभी सम्मिलित हैं। दुनिया में स्वतंत्रता, पिछड़ापन, कट्टरपन और सत्यप्रियता के बीच ये संघर्ष नया नहीं है। देखना यह है कि विजय किसकी होती है। धार्मिक समूह, कट्टर एकीकरण जो जीवन के प्रत्येक विभाग पर हावी होना चाहता है उसके अत्यधिक विरोधी हैं। क्योंकि वह सामाजिक जीवन से धर्म को समाप्त करना अत्यंत आवश्यक समझता है। दूसरी ओर एकीकरण के कट्टरपंथी ये समझते हैं कि धर्म के प्रभाव से स्वाधीनता, शोध एवं उन्नति में बाधा पड़ती है। न्याय की बात यह है कि दोनों पक्ष हद से गुज़र जाने का शिकार हैं और संतुलन से काम नहीं लेते हैं।

3

बहु भाषिता

प्रो. इम्तियाज़ हसनैन

विश्व के अधिकतर देशों में एक से अधिक भाषाएँ बोली जाती हैं। अनुमान है कि इस समय विश्व के दो सौ देशों में 6000 भाषाओं से लोग अपने जीवन की दिनचर्या का कार्य चलाते हैं। जहाँ केवल एक ही भाषा का चलन है वहाँ भी स्वाद बदलने के लिये क्षेत्रीय बोलियों का सहारा लेना पड़ता है। अधिक भाषाओं वाले देशों में बहुत से लोगों की मातृ भाषा भी एक से अधिक होती हैं।

द्विभाष्या या बहुभाषा के प्रयोग ने व्यक्ति और समाज दोनों को विभिन्न प्रकार से प्रभावित किया है। जब कोई व्यक्ति एक या एक से अधिक भाषाएँ बोलता और समझता है तो यह प्रश्न उठता है कि ये भाषाएँ उसने कैसे और कब सीखीं। क्या उसने बचपन में या उसके पश्चात सीखा, उनके प्रभाव उस पर क्या पड़े, बोलने-लिखने, पढ़ने में उसे क्या लाभ हुआ। इसी प्रकार किसी समाज में दो या अधिक भाषाओं का स्थान, प्रयोग, प्रसिद्धि और उनके धार्मिक एवं सामाजिक प्रभाव भी विशेष महत्व रखते हैं।

विश्व के अधिकतर देशों में विभिन्न भाषाओं का प्रयोग और उनका रिवाज दो प्रकार से हुआ। या तो इन देशों में यह भाषाएँ क्षेत्रीय आधार पर उपस्थिति थीं और उन्हें केन्द्रीय स्तर पर स्वीकार कर लिया गया जैसे कनाडा। यह आवश्यक नहीं कि उस देश में हर व्यक्ति एक से अधिक भाषाएँ बोलता या जानता हो। उन्नीसवीं शताब्दी बल्कि बीसवीं शताब्दी के आरंभ तक यह समझा जाता था कि दो भाषाओं या उससे अधिक का प्रयोग सदाचार के विपरीत, अविश्सनीय एवं खर्चीला है और बुद्धिमत्ता के आधार पर इनको रद्द कर देना चाहिये। बीसवीं सदी के अंत तक इस प्रकार की नकारात्मक सोच रखने में रोपर्टमरडूक जैसे प्रसिद्ध व्यक्ति ने भारत में एक से अधिक भाषाओं और उनके प्रयोग की निंदा करते हुये यहाँ तक कह डाला कि भारत की खंडता और पिछड़ेपन का कारण यही भाषाओं की अधिकता है जबकि इसकी तुलना में अंग्रेज़ी बोलने

वाली जनता अर्थात् जनसंख्या एकता एवं उन्नति की ओर अग्रसर है। आश्चर्य इस बात पर है कि संचार एवं प्रसार क्षेत्र में ऐसे प्रसिद्ध एवं महत्त्वपूर्ण व्यक्ति ने एक देश- एक भाषा के नारे को दोहराया और इस कठोर वास्तविकता को बिल्कुल भुला दिया कि ये अन्यायपूर्ण व्यवहार देश एवं विदेश के अल्पसंख्यकों के लिये बड़ा दुखदायी और ग़लत होगा।

किन्तु अब ये नकारात्मक सोच तेज़ी से बदल रही है और दो या उससे अधिक भाषाओं की लोकप्रियता में बढोत्तरी हो रही है और इसके राजनीतिक एवं शैक्षिक लाभ को खुलकर स्वीकार किया जा रहा है। भाषाओं की खोज और उनके सांस्कृतिक एवं वैचारिक प्रभाव में धर्म एवं सभ्यताएँ बड़ी रुचि ले रही हैं। किसी भी देश या क्षेत्र में व्यक्ति और समूहों के मध्य प्रचार एवं प्रसार बहुत महत्व रखता है। विशेषकर भारत जैसे देश में जहाँ विभिन्न धर्मों, संस्कृतियों एवं रीतिरिवाज के मानने वाले रहते हैं वहाँ एक दूसरे तक बात पहुँचाने और उनके हालात को जानने के लिये आवश्यक है कि यहाँ लोग एक से अधिक भाषाओं का प्रयोग करें। इस प्रकार से देश की एकता, शक्ति एवं न्याय को बराबर एवं सामाजिक-समानता को बनाये रखा जा सकता है। इस वातावरण में कोई विशेष समूह या भाषा इतनी शक्तिशाली नहीं हो सकती कि दूसरों को हर तरह से दबाकर अपने आधीन रख सकें। भाषाई द्वेष एवं पक्षपात की घटनाएँ, इतिहास बताता है कि भारत और विश्व के दूसरे देशों में उस समय हुईं जब सत्ता पक्ष के गिरोह ने अल्पसंख्यक होने के बावजूद अपनी भाषा सीखने पर दूसरे समूहों को मजबूर किया और ये बहुत कम देखने में आया कि कमजोर वर्ग की भाषा सत्ताधारियों ने खुशी से सीखना स्वीकार किया हो। जैसे फिनलैण्ड में डच एवं स्वीड् नागरिकों को ज़बरदस्ती फिनलैण्ड की भाषा सीखनी पड़ी जबकि स्वयं फिनलैण्ड के नागरिकों ने उनकी भाषाओं को ध्यान देने के योग्य नहीं समझा।

भारत में असंख्य संप्रदाय, भाषाएँ, लिपि एवं विभिन्न जाति व रंग वाले लोग सदियों से साथ-साथ रह रहे हैं। हिन्दू, बुद्ध, जैन और सिख इसी धरती से उपजे हैं, बाहर से आने वाले धर्मों में ईसाई, इस्लाम, यहूदी और मज़ुकियत महत्वपूर्ण हैं। इनके अतिरिक्त देश में नामालूम कितने आदिवासी धर्म, आस्थाएँ और विश्वास के मानने वाले लोग रहते हैं। यहाँ के भाषायी मानचित्र पर हिन्द आर्या, द्रविण, आस्ट्रो एशियाई, तिब्बत व बरमन और अंडमानी भाषाओं के

परिवार दिखाई देते हैं। सामने से ये बात अनोखी दिखती है कि भारत की राष्ट्रीय एकता और संयुक्त संस्कृति के बावजूद सैकड़ों वर्षों से भाषा के ये मतभेद अपनी परंपराओं के साथ बाक़ी हैं। इसका समर्थन जनगणना के रिकार्ड और सामाजिक एवं भाषायी बुद्धजीवियों के शोध से होती है। अंग्रेज़ी शासन में जार्जग्रियरसन ने भारत की भाषाओं का परीक्षण कर के 1898 में एक विस्तृत रिपोर्ट तैयार की थी।

ये बात रुचिपूर्ण है कि आज की भारतीय भाषाओं में अधिकतर की लिपि ब्राह्मी लिपि से निकली है। जिसका पहला नमूना तीसरी शताब्दी पूर्व ईसा मसीह अशोक के ज़माने के स्तूपों में मिलता है इसके पश्चात हिन्दुकाल में लिपि के दो नमूने कुछ परिवर्तनों के साथ उत्तर भारत और दक्षिण भारत में प्रचलित हुए। उत्तरी लिपि में चौथी पांचवी शताब्दी में शारदा, लिंडा, गुरुमुखि, टकरी, कतेला लिपियाँ उत्पन्न हुईं। इसके पश्चात् कैथी, मूदी लिपियाँ आयीं और फिर नागरी लिपि का जन्म हुआ। दक्षिण भारत में ब्राह्मी लिपि से कन्नड़, तेलगू, तमिल, मलयालम भाषाओं की लिपियाँ निकलीं। भारत में अरब की कूफी और नस्ख़ लिपियाँ मुसलमानों के साथ आयीं। हमारे संविधान में जिन भाषाओं को स्थान दिया गया है उनकी पहचान उनकी लिपि से की जाती है। इसके अतिरिक्त रोमन लिपि भी प्रयोग में है।

ये वास्तविकता है कि भारत और यहाँ के समाज की विशेषता यह रही है कि यहाँ कई भाषाएँ हर काल में प्रचलित रही हैं। इतिहासकारों के अनुसार हिन्द आर्या, द्रविड़, आस्ट्रिक और साइनो-तिब्बत भाषाओं का प्रयोग शताब्दियों से होता आ रहा है। इससे पता चलता है कि भारत भाषाओं के लिहाज़ से एक विशाल स्वरूप रखता है। यहाँ भाषाओं की अधिकता का अर्थ दो भिन्न प्रकार से निकाला जाता है। प्रथम तो यह कि विशेष भाषाओं को महत्व के आधार पर सरकारी स्तर दिया गया और शेष भाषाएँ यहाँ के नागरिक अपने-अपने क्षेत्रों में प्रयोग करते हैं। 1991 की जनगणना के अनुसार 1574 मातृ भाषाएँ यहाँ पर हैं। हमारे संविधान ने 22 भाषाओं को राष्ट्र भाषा स्वीकार किया है। साहित्य अकादमी ने ये स्थान 24 भाषाओं को दिया है। जबकि आल इण्डिया रेडियो से प्रचार व प्रसार 80 भाषाओं में होता है। भाषाओं की इस अधिकता ने देश की रंग-बिरंगी संस्कृति और एक दूसरे को समझने का बड़ा अच्छा अवसर प्रदान किया है। राष्ट्रीय संपर्क के लिये हिन्दुस्तानी भाषा बनी है। जो दूसरी

भाषाओं के शब्दों के कारण खिचड़ी की तरह है जिसे देश के अधिकतर लोग समझते हैं। ये प्रसन्नता एवं गर्व की बात है कि हमारे देश की सभी भाषाओं को अपने क्षेत्र में बढ़ने और उन्नति करने का अवसर प्राप्त है और इनमें कोई टकराव नज़र नहीं आता।

इन भाषाओं से सभी प्रकार की मालूमात और आवश्यक बातें देश के दूर-दूर तक बसने वालों तक पहुँचाई जा सकती हैं। भाषाओं की अधिकता एवं व्यापकता से प्रचार व प्रसार, शिक्षा, मनोरंजन एवं शोध के विभागों में बड़ी व्यापकता एवं गहराई उत्पन्न हुई है जो कोई साधारण बात नहीं है।

भाषाओं की अधिकता अब हमारे समाज एवं देश की विशेषता बन चुकी है इसलिए आवश्यक है कि इस महत्वपूर्ण माध्यम से पूरा लाभ उठाया जाये और अनावश्यक रूप से देश की भाषाओं में आपस में तुलना या संघर्ष की स्थिति न आने दी जाये। यह कार्य हमारे बुद्धिजीवियों, प्रशासन, कानून, समाज सेवकों एवं मीडिया का है। यह अच्छी तरह जान लेना चाहिए कि भाषाओं की अधिकता ने बहुत सी शैक्षिक, भाषा संबंधी, राजनीतिक एवं आर्थिक उलझने भी पैदा की हैं। जिसको आपसी सूझबूझ से हल किया जा सकता है। उदाहरण के लिये अंग्रेज़ी भाषा को प्रस्तुत किया जा सकता है। जो इस समय विश्व की अनेक भाषाओं की उन्नति का महत्वपूर्ण कार्य कर रही है। इस बारे में लातीनी और संस्कृत भाषा का नाम भी लिया जा सकता है। जिनकी गणना मृत या मृतप्राय भाषाओं में की जाती है। भाषा एवं ज्ञान के क्षेत्र में अनुभव और अध्ययन से ये ज्ञात हुआ है कि एक भाषा सीखने वाले विद्यार्थियों की तुलना में अनेक भाषाएँ सीखने वाले विद्यार्थी ने अच्छी योग्यता का प्रदर्शन किया और अधिक अंक प्राप्त किये। इन विद्यार्थियों ने शब्दों की ध्वनि, अर्थ नाम और उनसे संबंधी विस्तृत जानकारी शीघ्र सीख ली। अतः यह कहा जा सकता है कि एक से अधिक भाषा सीखने वाले विद्यार्थी की योग्यता एक भाषा सीखने वालों से कहीं बेहतर होती है।

अंत में इस बात की ओर ध्यान आकर्षित करना भी आवश्यक है कि दो भाषाओं की सरकारी क्षत्रछाया एवं सहायता की नीति जो हमारे संविधान के अनुसार देश में जारी है उसके अंतर्गत हिन्दी और अंग्रेज़ी को दूसरी क्षेत्रीय भाषाओं की तुलना में जो विशेष ध्यान दिया जा रहा है वह देश की दूसरी भाषाओं की उन्नति और विकास के लिये हानिकारक है। इससे देश के भाषायी

एवं सांस्कृतिक विकास पर अच्छा प्रभाव नहीं होगा। इस कारण बुद्धजीवियों एवं सरकार चलाने वालों को इस ओर ध्यान देकर सभी भाषाओं को फलने फूलने और उन्नति का अवसर देना चाहिए। ताकि देश में आंतरिक संघर्ष न फैले और उसकी एकता बनी रहे।

4

राष्ट्रीय एकता के आयाम

डॉ. आर.एस. वार्ष्णेय

राष्ट्रीय एकता एक बड़ा व्यापक शब्द है और इसके अर्थ को समझने के लिये आवश्यक है कि इसके तीन महत्त्वपूर्ण आयामों को पूर्ण रूप से समझा जाये।

1. सर्व प्रथम हमें राष्ट्रीय एकता की कल्पना और उससे जुड़ी समस्याओं के बारे में समाज शास्त्रियों और समाज सेवकों के विचारों एवं भावनाओं को जानना चाहिए।
2. दूसरे नंबर पर उन घटनाओं, हालात, ऐतिहासिक एवं सामाजिक परिदृश्य को देखना चाहिए जिसका सामना हमारे देश और देशवासियों ने किया है। यह एक ऐसा मिला जुला दृश्य है जिसमें राष्ट्रीय मेल-मिलाप के साथ आपस के लड़ाई-झगड़ों, पूर्वाग्रहों और अमानवीय बर्ताव के चित्र दिखाई देते हैं। जिन्होंने हमारे देश को प्रगति एवं शक्ति के रास्ते से हटाकर कमज़ोर और बदनाम किया है।
3. हमें उन कोशिशों और प्रयत्नों का अध्ययन करना चाहिए जो हालात को सुधारने और राष्ट्रीय एकता को बढ़ाने के लिये किये गये। लेखों, भाषणों और व्यक्तिगत एवं सामूहिक प्रयत्नों का जायज़ा लेना चाहिए कि इस उद्‌देश्य को पाने में कहाँ तक सफलता मिली है।

राष्ट्रीय एकता का दायरा बड़ा व्यापक है। समाज की प्रगति, देश-प्रेम, राष्ट्रीय धरोहर, प्रमुख ऐतिहासिक घटनाओं और हमारे देशवासियों के शानदार कारनामों ने इसे बढ़ाया और जीवन के विभिन्न भागों पर असर डाला है। हमारा यह कर्त्तव्य है कि हर मूल्य पर इसकी सुरक्षा करें और इसकी आवश्यकता को पूरी तरह समझें।

राष्ट्रीय एकता का अर्थ उसके विभिन्न आयाम और नकारात्मक एवं सकारात्मक प्रभाव :

इस दृष्टिकोण की नींव देशभक्ति, मानवीयता, सदाचार, आपसी मेल-मिलाप और विभिन्न स्तरों पर किये गये अच्छे कार्यों और अनुशासन पर है। अगर हमारे देश में राष्ट्रीय एवं सामाजिक स्तर पर प्रगति, आपसी मेल-मिलाप, क्षमा जैसी अच्छी बातों के सीखने, मिलजुलकर रहने और धैर्य धारण करने की भावनाएँ उत्पन्न हो जायें और सभी नागरिक इसका पालन करने लगें तो हमको एकता और भाईचारे की अमूल्य दौलत प्राप्त हो जायेगी। इसके विपरीत अगर पक्षपात, एक दूसरे से घृणा, जलन, तोड़फोड़, अलग रहने और मेलमिलाप से दूर भागने, धर्म, भाषा और संस्कृति के मामले में कट्टरपन और पक्षपात का ढंग अपनाया जायेगा तो राष्ट्रीय एकता चूर-चूर हो जायेगी और देश विघटन के मार्ग पर आ जायेगा।

भाई चारे के लिये ज़रूरी है कि हम अपने देश में सामाजिक और राजनीतिक स्तर पर अच्छा शासन और समझदार नेतृत्व क़ायम करें और इतिहास एवं समाजशास्त्र की रोशनी में देश से वफादारी और अपने देशवासियों से सहानुभूति रखें। कानून का आदर करें, धर्म की सच्ची शिक्षा का पालन करें। धर्म, दर्शन और जनहित में शिक्षा के प्रबंध और मीडिया के सुप्रभाव से जनजीवन को लाभ पहुँचाएँ। जिससे वह राष्ट्रीय एकता और देश की शानदार सभ्यता एवं संस्कृति, शैक्षिक एवं ऐतिहासिक धरोहर का सम्मान कर सकें। इस श्रृंखला में मनोवैज्ञानिक रूप से नस्ल, धर्म, भाषा, रीति रिवाज, जातपात एवं क्षेत्रीय विशेषताएँ बड़ी उपयोगी होती हैं। मगर शर्त यह है कि उनको सही और सकारात्मक रूप में लोगों के सामने लाया जाये क्योंकि नस्ल, धर्म, जातपात, भाषा, परिवार, क़बीलों और इलाकों को कट्टरपन, पक्षपात और नफ़रत बढ़ाने के लिये आसानी से प्रयोग किया जा सकता है। हमारे देश में इसके दुखदायी उदाहरण भी मौजूद हैं। यह कार्य हमारे राजनीतिक एवं धार्मिक लीडर, पार्टियाँ, प्रशासन, समाजसेवक, व्यापारी एवं शिक्षा, नौकरी और खेतीबाड़ी तथा विभिन्न पेशों और कामों में लगे लोग और संगठन सभी कर सकते हैं। मीडिया, पार्लियामेन्ट, मन्दिर, मस्जिद, गिरजाघर, गुरुद्वारा, फौज, पुलिस सबसे आगे बढ़कर कुछ लोगों के कट्टरपन, दुर्व्यवहार, स्वार्थ और देशद्रोहिता के नकारात्मक और बुरे प्रभाव को दूर कर सकते हैं।

हमारे देश के लोग अपने धर्म, भाषा, रीति-रिवाज और देश से प्रेम करते हैं यह राष्ट्रीय एकता के लिये बहुत अच्छी बात है और इसकी मदद से एकता

और भाई चारे को बढ़ाया जा सकता है। इसके साथ यह भी आवश्यक है कि हमारा समाज धार्मिक, सांस्कृतिक, राजनीतिक और मानवतावादी रुझान पर चिंतन करे और डिक्टेटेरशिप, पक्षपात, विभाजन एवं भेदभाव की ताकत को बढ़ने और फैलने से रोके।

यहाँ यह प्रश्न उठता है कि राष्ट्रीय एकता क्या चीज है। वह किसके लिये है और उसे कैसे क़ायम किया और फैलाया जा सकता है। राष्ट्रीय एकता एक ऐसी भावना और ताक़त है जो हमारे देश और समाज के विभिन्न भागों को एकता में अनेकता के प्रारंभिक उसूल के तहत जोड़े रखती है और देश-प्रेम एवं वफादारी को बढ़ाती है। यह हमारे देश, यहाँ के रहने वालों, यहाँ की सभ्यता एवं संस्कृति, इतिहास और मानवतावादी मूल्यों का अटूट हिस्सा है। जो सबके लिये लाभदायक एवं आवश्यक है। इसको विभिन्न संस्थाओं एवं संघटनों के द्वारा सुरक्षित रखा जा सकता है।

पहले यह समझ लेना चाहिये कि राष्ट्र का क्या अर्थ है। दुर्भाग्यवश राजनीति के पंडितों, इतिहासकारों एवं समाजशास्त्रियों ने इसके अलग-अलग अर्थ निकाले हैं। जिसके कारण इसे समझने में परेशानी होती है। कहीं राजनीति, कहीं धर्म और कहीं जाति या भाषा के आधार पर 'राष्ट्र' के ऐसे अर्थ निकाले गये हैं जिनके कारण वह असलियत से दूर हो गये हैं। राष्ट्र बहुत से भागों और खण्डों से मिलकर बना है। जैसे कानून, प्रजातंत्र, शासन इत्यादि। लीग आफ नेशन्स ने 'राष्ट्र' की परिभाषा यह दी थी कि इसमें वह तमाम हुकूमतें शामिल हैं जो स्वतंत्र हों, अपने तौर पर हुकूमत करने या समाजी तरक़्की और अच्छे व्यवहार की मालिक हो। बहरहाल राष्ट्रीयता का अर्थ राजनीतिक एकता, आज़ाद हुकूमत के बनाने और ऊँचे मूल्यों को प्रस्तुत करता है।

'राष्ट्र' और 'सरकार' के बीच अन्तर करना कठिन है क्योंकि बुद्धिजीवियों ने इस बारे में कोई साफ़ बात नहीं कही है। कहीं दोनों को एक कहा गया है, कहीं अलग-अलग पहचान की गई है और गोलमोल अंदाज में दोनों शब्दों का प्रयोग किया गया है। सत्य यह है कि राष्ट्र हुकूमत से अधिक विस्तृत अर्थ रखता है वह विभिन्न वर्गों की आबादी पर निर्भर होता है जो किसी भौगोलिक क्षेत्र में आबाद होती है और विभिन्न प्रकार के काम करती है। कानून और प्रशासन की बालादस्ती के लिये उसी के अंतर्गत एक संगठन 'हुकूमत' होता

है जो राष्ट्र की पहचान के लिये शक्ति का स्रोत होता है। जो लोग यह कहते हैं कि राष्ट्र के लिये हुकूमत का होना आवश्यक नहीं वह गलती पर हैं। राष्ट्र किसी क्षेत्र में आबाद उन लोगों को कहते हैं जो अपने ऊपर हुकूमत करने के लिये शासन तंत्र को बनाते हैं। जो उस क्षेत्र में शांति और जीवन की सुविधाएँ प्रदान करता है। राष्ट्र की पहचान और उसके निर्माण में नस्ल, धर्म, भाषा, इतिहास और सबसे बढ़कर जनमत का बड़ा दखल होता है। जो एक समाज का सदस्य होने के साथ-साथ अपने को एक राष्ट्र बनाने का आंदोलन चलाते हैं और अपने ऊपर राज्य करने के लिये शासन तंत्र का निर्माण करते हैं। इस तरह से हम समाज, राष्ट्र और शासन के विभिन्न स्थानों को और उनके प्रभाव को समझ सकते हैं। राष्ट्र के लिये आवश्यक है कि उसका एक विशेष भौगोलिक क्षेत्र हो, उसके पास प्रबंध के लिये जनमत के अनुसार एक शासन तंत्र हो उसकी ऐतिहासिक एवं सांस्कृतिक विशेषतायें हों, कानून का उच्च स्थान और सभ्यता एवं मूल्यों की परंपरा हो और वहाँ के रहने वालों में एकता और मेलजोल पाया जाये। उसकी एक मिली जुली भाषा हो, एक राष्ट्रीय ध्वज हो, एक राष्ट्रीय गान हो, आर्थिक सुविधाएँ हों और मानसिक एवं भावनात्मक रूप से देश से वफादारी और कुछ ऐसे राष्ट्रीय उद्देश्य और उच्च स्तर हो जिनसे दुनिया में उसकी पहचान हो सके। इन सारी बातों में इतिहास व राजनीति के आधार पर निरंतर प्रगति एवं बदलाव होता रहता है। राष्ट्र के अंदर एक से अधिक समाज हो सकते हैं जिनकी बुनियाद रीति-रिवाज, परंपरा और जीवन शैली पर होती है।

यह भी याद रखना चाहिए कि राष्ट्रीयता का आभास और सुरक्षा अत्यंत आवश्यक है नहीं तो उसका परिणाम गृहयुद्ध, खूनखराबा, गुलामी और पतन होता है इसी लिये हम सबको अपने देश की सुरक्षा, स्वतंत्रता, राष्ट्रीय ध्वज, राष्ट्रीय भाषा और राष्ट्रीय धरोहर का विशेष आदर करना चाहिए और इन सबका वफादार रहना चाहिए।

जो लोग ऐसा नहीं करते और इन रेखाओं पर नहीं सोचते वह देश से दुश्मनी करते हैं और उनसे देश एवं राष्ट्र को तबाही व बर्बादी का ख़तरा रहता है।

उच्च शासन और आज़ादी के साथ ये भी जनता की ज़िम्मेदारी है कि वह इसकी सुरक्षा करे अर्थात शासक या कोई व्यक्ति या गिरोह अगर भ्रष्टाचार,

रिश्वत या देशद्रोही काम करे तो कोशिश करके (जिसमें प्रदर्शन, धरना और बाईकाट इत्यादि भी सम्मिलित है) ऐसे शासन को हटाने या हटने पर मजबूर कर दें और ऐसे लोगों को कड़ी सजा दिलवायें।

राष्ट्रीय एकता के लिये यह भी आवश्यक है कि समाज और उसमें सम्मिलित सभी वर्ग और संस्थाएँ देश की राजनीतिक, सांस्कृतिक और सामाजिक एकता को बाक़ी रखें। इसका अर्थ यह नहीं कि वह सब एक हो जायें और अपना अस्तित्व समाप्त कर लें। उनको चाहिए कि वह अपने कार्य-कलापों को राष्ट्रीय एकता और देश की प्रगति के अंतर्गत करें और मिलजुल कर रहें, एक दूसरे से मेल-मिलाप रखें, दूसरों की भावनाओं का आदर करें, मिली-जुली सभ्यता एवं संस्कृति बहुत अच्छा उपहार है जिस पर भारत को गर्व है।

राष्ट्रीय एकता के लिये आवश्यक है कि हम अपने भाषा संबंधी, धार्मिक और सामाजिक विरोधों को राष्ट्रीय तानेबाने में स्थान दें। यह कार्य थोड़े धैर्य और सहन शक्ति द्वारा हो सकता है। राष्ट्रीय एकता को इन विरोधों के बावजूद बनाए रखा जा सकता है। जिसका सुबूत हमारा इतिहास और सामाजिक जीवन चाहे वह गाँव में हो या शहर में, दे रहा है। हमको टकराव और बड़े होने की भावना से बचना चाहिए। संगठित होकर सबको यह प्रयत्न करना चाहिए कि अपनी विशेष परम्पराओं और जीवन शैली को राष्ट्रीय धारा में समा दिया जाय तथा नफ़रत एवं दूरी को मिटाया जाय, यह कार्य कठिन अवश्य है किन्तु असम्भव नहीं।

स्वतंत्रता के उपरान्त हमारे देश और समाज में इस सम्बन्ध में बहुत कार्य हुआ है, अच्छा भी और बुरा भी। यह समस्या बहुत बड़ी है। एक ओर हमारे नेताओं, मीडिया, धार्मिक एवं सामाजिक कार्यकर्ताओं ने राष्ट्रीय एकता और भाईचारे के लिऐ बहुत कोशिशें कीं, त्याग किये और इस आवश्यक कार्य की ओर देश वासियों को आकर्षित किया। मगर उसी के साथ दुर्भाग्यवश कुछ लोगों ने जिनमें राजनीतिक पार्टियाँ, लीडर, धार्मिक और सामाजिक संस्थाएँ, मीडिया, शिक्षित लोग, सभी सम्मिलित थे, विरोध और नफ़रत की भावनाओं को भड़काया और फैलाया। भाषा, धर्म, क्षेत्र, रीति-रिवाज, जाति-पाति और राजनीतिक बातों को लेकर साम्प्रदायिक दंगे, लूटमार, तबाही और बर्बादी की ऐसी घटनाएँ हुयीं जिनसे हिन्दुस्तान की बड़ी बदनामी हुई और प्रगति की दौड़ में हम पीछे रह गये। यह याद रखना चाहिए कि हमने स्वतन्त्रता बड़ी मुश्किल

से अच्छी ख़ासी कीमत और कुरबानी देकर प्राप्त की है। हिन्दुस्तान जैसे बड़े देश में जहाँ विभिन्न प्रकार की भाषाएँ, धर्म, रीति-रिवाज पाये जाते हैं। एकता और सबको एक साथ जोड़ने का काम आसान नहीं था। भारत वर्ष के स्वतंत्र शासन ने इस कठिन समस्या को हल करने के अनेक प्रयास किये। एकता लाने के लिए उच्च स्तरीय कानून बनाया गया। सुविधाओं को प्रगति के लिए, प्रयोग करने के लिए अच्छी योजनाएँ तैयार की गयीं। बटवारे के बाद शैक्षिक, सामाजिक एवं आर्थिक पिछड़ेपन को दूर करने के लिये प्रभावी योजनाएँ बनाई गयीं। इस मार्ग में बड़ी बाधाएँ आयीं। देश की बर्बाद हुई अर्थव्यवस्था और बिगड़ी हुई नैतिक एवं सामाजिक हालत को सुधारना आसान काम नहीं था। फिर से बसाने, राष्ट्रीयता और एकता के निर्माण में असमानता, ग़रीबी, अशिक्षा, तंगनज़री और पक्षपात के कारण बड़ी कठिनाईयां हुयीं। फिर भी इन प्रयासों का अच्छा परिणाम निकला और देश के सामाजिक व आर्थिक जीवन में बड़ा बदलाव आया मगर अब भी समस्याएँ पूर्ण रूप से हल नहीं हो पाई हैं। अभी और काम और ध्यान की आवश्यकता है जिसमें सभी नागरिकों को भाग लेना चाहिए।

राष्ट्रीय एकता के मार्ग में बड़ी रुकावटें निम्नलिखित हैं

1. देश में कुछ ऐसे वर्ग, लोग और संगठन हैं जो अपनी विशेष सांस्कृतिक धरोहर जैसे धर्म, भाषा, रीति-रिवाज की आड़ लेकर राष्ट्रीय एकता एंव भाईचारे के विरुद्ध हैं और अन्याय और हिंसा के रास्ते पर चल रहे हैं। यह लोग अपने को बड़ा साबित करके देश को अपनी इच्छानुसार ग़लत रास्ते पर ले जाना चाहते हैं।
2. राष्ट्रीय एकता के विरोधी पक्षपात एवं संकीर्णता से काम लेकर प्रजातंत्र एवं धर्म निरपेक्षता के विरुद्ध आंदोलन चला रहे हैं। ऐतिहासिक घटनाओं को तोड़मोड़कर, झूठे आरोप लगाकर हमारे उज्ज्वल इतिहास को बदनाम कर रहे हैं। जसे कुछ कट्टरपंथी हिन्दू, मुसलमानों को विदेशी, क्रूर, जालिम ठहराते हैं और मुसलमान राजाओं के अत्याचार की कहानियाँ अतिश्योक्ति के साथ सुनाकर जनता में जोश फैलाते और उसे गुमराह करते हैं। वह एक विशेष संस्कृति और शासन व्यवस्था (हिन्दुत्व) को

देश पर थोपना चाहते हैं। दूसरी ओर कुछ कट्टरवादी मुसलमान हिन्दुओं के धर्म, इतिहास और रीतिरिवाज को तरह-तरह से बदनाम करने का प्रयास करते हैं। और उनका साथ देने को बुरा कहते हैं। दुर्भाग्यवश बुद्धिजीवियों और मीडिया का एक बड़ा वर्ग इन देशद्रोही विचारों की पैरवी संगठित रूप से कर रहा है।

3. एक और दुःखद दृष्टिकोण देश में कुछ खतरों और अंदेशों की बिना पर साम्प्रदायिकता और अलगाववाद को हवा दे रहा है। जैसे कुछ नेता, पार्टियाँ, संगठन और समाचार पत्र इन बातों को उछालते हैं कि देश में धर्म परिवर्तन का बड़ा ज़ोर है, विशेष धर्म या सम्प्रदाय की जनसंख्या में तेज़ी से बढ़ोत्तरी हो रही है, या नफ़रत और दुश्मनी के कारण साम्प्रदायिकता, खूनख़राबा और तबाही व बर्बादी का डर हर समय लगा रहता है। वह यह भी आरोप लगाते हैं कि सरकार इन मामलों में मुंह भराई और खामोशी से काम चलाती है।

इस प्रकार का विषैला प्रचार साम्प्रदायिक एकता और भाईचारे के लिए विष के समान है। हम सबको चाहिए कि इसको सफल न होने दें।

5

समानतावादी समाज में बराबरी का अर्थ

प्रो. अब्दुल रहीम पी. वीजापुर

शताब्दियों से ईश्वर के अवतारों, धर्म गुरुओं, दर्शनशास्त्रियों, बुद्धिजीवियों और राजनीतिक समझ रखने वालों में बहस चली आ रही है कि समानतावादी समाज क्या चीज़ है और इस का निर्माण कैसे किया जा सकता है। इसके नियम क्या हैं। समानता के कार्य का स्वरूप क्या है। इसको लागू करने के लिए क्या केवल सकारात्मक कार्यवाही करना आवश्यक है या अंतर और दबाव से भी काम लेना ज़रूरी है। आज भी मानव अधिकारों के वकील इन प्रश्नों में उलझे हुए हैं। सबसे पहले हमको समझ लेना चाहिए कि समानतावादी समाज और समानता के असली अर्थ क्या है? यह शब्द अंग्रेज़ी भाषा में फ्रांसीसी से आये हैं जिनका अर्थ है कि सभी नागरिकों को किसी देश में जन्म लेने के बाद एक-जैसे राजनीतिक, सामाजिक, आर्थिक और शहरी अधिकार प्राप्त हों। वह शासन, धर्म और कानून की दृष्टि में समान समझे जाते हैं।

आज के राजनीतिक वातावरण में नागरिकों की बराबरी की समस्या बहुत महत्त्वपूर्ण है। असमानता और ऊँच-नीच देश में बिखराव, अशांति यहाँ तक कि इंक़लाब ला सकती है किन्तु समानता के दृष्टि-कोण के कार्यान्वन के संबंध में विरोधी विचार पाये जाते हैं। लोगों में समानता, सुविधा, प्रतिभा, सुधार, आदर, सम्मान और एक जैसे अवसरों के मिलने के द्वारा लाई जा सकती है। इस बारे में टकराव या किसी एक के चुनाव का फैसला करना पड़ता है। प्रसिद्ध फ्रांसीसी विद्वान रूसो का कहना है कि मनुष्यों में असमानता दो प्रकार की पाई जाती है। प्रथम तो प्राकृतिक रूप में, जिसका संबंध आयु, स्वास्थ्य, शारीरिक एवं मानसिक शक्तियों से होता है और दूसरा धन दौलत, ताकत, आदर व सम्मान के अनुसार होता है। पहले प्रकार की असमानता प्रकृति की ओर से होती है और दूसरी मनुष्यों की बनाई हुई। इस प्रकार की असमानता उस समय के समाज, शासन और न्याय के ग़लत व्यवहार का परिणाम 1789 में फ्रांस में देखा गया जिसके

उपरान्त वहां नागरिकों के अधिकार का चार्टर तैयार किया गया। इस बारे में रूसो की ज़बान से यह इंक़लाब भरा नारा निकला "सभी मनुष्य समानता और स्वतंत्रता के अधिकार लेकर पैदा होते हैं मगर समाज उनको असमानता और ऊँच-नीच की जंजीरों में जकड़ लेता है।"

इस बारे में कुछ और प्रसिद्ध राजनीतिक, विद्वानों के विचार इस प्रकार हैं –

आरनेसन के अनुसार राजनीतिक समानता, प्रजातांत्रिक शहरी अधिकार से बढ़कर व्यापक और शक्तिशाली होती है जिसमें प्रत्येक नागरिक को एक समान राजनीतिक एवं आर्थिक अधिकार प्राप्त होते हैं। जिसका आधार जन सेवा एवं सुधार के साधन और योग्यताओं को अपनी इच्छानुसार प्रयोग करने पर होता है। एक दूसरे विद्वान जानरावल ने न्याय पर आधारित समानता का दृष्टिकोण प्रस्तुत किया। उसने तीन नियमों का सहारा लिया।

1. राजनीति में भाग लेने, विचारों की स्वतंत्रता, धर्म की स्वतंत्रता और कानून के समक्ष बराबरी का अधिकार।
2. योग्यता बढ़ाने, पद और ज़िम्मेदारी प्राप्त करने के अवसरों की समानता।
3. समाज के पिछड़े वर्ग को लाभ पहुँचाने के लिये उनके साथ कुछ अलग करने की आज्ञा।

इनका कहना है कि यह तीनों नियम समाज के कल्याण के लिये एक जंजीर की कड़ियों की तरह हैं और यह आवयश्यक है कि कमजोर कड़ी को ठीक करके हमेशा ज़ंजीर को सही और मजबूत अवस्था में रखा जाये।

रोनॉल्ड डारकिन के अनुसार समानता, भलाई के कार्यों और उनके साधनों के अच्छे बटवारे पर निर्भर होती है। इसके दो रूप हैं। पहले में लोगों में संसाधनों का बटवारा इस प्रकार क़िया जाता है कि उसका हर एक को समान हिस्सा मिले। इस बारे में लोगों की पसंद और हौसलों को ध्यान में रखा जाता है। दूसरे रूप में लोगों में बराबर-बराबर संसाधनों का बटवारा यह मानकर किया जाता है कि वह सब हर प्रकार से बराबर हैं। वह स्वयं दूसरे रूप का समर्थन करते हैं भारत के नोबेल पुरस्कार विजेता विद्वान अमृत्यसेन ने समानता के सभी दृष्टिकोणों का गहन अध्ययन करने के उपरांत यह बताया कि हर दृष्टिकोण

में कुछ न कुछ कमी पायी जाती है इसलिये इन सबको मिलाकर उन्होंने एक दृष्टिकोण बराबरी के आधार पर योग्यता का बनाया जिसके अनुसार लोग विभिन्न चीजों के प्रयोग से बराबरी का हिस्सा पा सकते हैं।

आज समाज में बराबरी लाने के लिये समाजवाद, प्रगतिवाद, मानवआधिकार और भलाई का विचार एवं आंदोलन संसार में मौजूद हैं जिनमें लोगों की कानूनी, सामाजिक, आर्थिक और राजनीतिक बराबरी के अधिकार दिये जाने का दावा किया जाता है। समाजवाद और प्रगतिवाद में निजी संपत्ति के स्थान पर राज्य को तमाम चीज़ों का मालिक मान लिया गया और व्यक्तियों को काम करने, सामाजिक सुरक्षा, शिक्षा, स्वास्थ्य और घर रखने के अधिकार की जमानत दी जाती है अतः सोवियत रूस में 1917 और 1991 के बीच इस नीति पर कार्य किया गया जो बड़ी हद तक सफल रहा किन्तु पूर्वी योरोप के दूसरे कम्यूनिस्ट देशों में ऐसा नहीं हुआ क्योंकि वहाँ राज्य ने शहरियों को राजनीतिक और धार्मिक अधिकारों की पूरी स्वतंत्रता नहीं दी। कुछ पूंजीवादी शासनों ने सामाजिक सुरक्षा और धार्मिक स्वतंत्रता के समान अधिकार अपने नागरिकों को इसलिए दिये ताकि वह कम्यूनिस्ट प्रकार का इन्क़लाब लाने के प्रयत्नों से दूर रहें।

विश्व के महान धर्मों में समानता की शिक्षा

दुनिया के बड़े धर्मों ईसाई, इस्लाम और हिन्दूमत में मनुष्यों की बराबरी को माना गया है। हिन्दू मत के उपनिषदों और भगवत गीता में इस आधारभूत विश्वास को प्रस्तुत किया गया है कि भगवान हर जगह है और हर वस्तु में है और उसके बनाये हुए मनुष्यों में कोई अंतर नहीं पाया जाता। जाति पांति का ज़ोर पकड़ने से पहले हिन्दू उपदेशों में सब धर्मों के एक होने और मानवता का एक कुटुम्ब होने का वर्णन अधिकता से मिलता है। ईसाईयों के दृष्टिकोण से बाइबिल में सभी स्त्रियों एवं पुरुषों के चाहे वह किसी नस्ली, आर्थिक या सामाजिक समूह से संबंध रखते हैं, हज़रत ईसा के मानने वाले और एक दूसरे के समान होने पर ज़ोर दिया गया है और यह कहा गया है कि भगवान सब मनुष्यों से समान रूप से प्रेम करता है और उनमें लिंग, जाति, पद के अनुसार कोई अंतर नहीं करता किन्तु दुख है कि हिन्दूमत और ईसाई धर्म दोनों में इन शिक्षाओं पर कार्य नहीं किया जाता और दलितों एवं औरतों के साथ अच्छा व्यवहार नहीं किया

जाता। इस्लाम ने बराबरी एवं विश्व परिवार की कल्पना को सब तक पहुँचाने का प्रयास किया। वह रंग, नस्ल या लिंग के आधार पर मनुष्यों में कोई अंतर नहीं करता। इस्लाम ने हर मनुष्य को चाहे वह मुसलमान हो या न हो अपने कानून के अंतर्गत बराबरी का स्थान दिया है। और जो मुसलमान नहीं है उनके अधिकारों को भी सुरक्षा प्रदान की है। अरफात के मैदान के अंतिम उपदेश में अल्लाह के अंतिम रसूल हज़रत मोहम्मद ने यह घोषणा की कि ऐ लोगो तुम्हारा ईश्वर एक है जिसने तुमको हज़रत आदम की औलाद में मिट्टी से पैदा किया। तुममें से किसी को रंग, नस्ल, दौलत या पद के आधार पर उच्चता प्राप्त नहीं क्योंकि इसका संबंध केवल अच्छे कार्यों से है। इस्लामी शासन और समाज ने संसार में मनुष्यों की समानता पर ज़ोर दिया जिसको आरनाल्ड-टायनबी एवं दूसरे इतिहासकारों और सामाजिक व राजनीतिक विचारकों ने स्वीकार किया। विवाह, पदों का बटवारा एवं महिलाओं के अधिकार के बारे में इस्लाम ने समानता के नियमों पर बड़े सुंदर ढंग से अमल किया है।

समानता, मानव अधिकार एवं अल्पसंख्यकों के अधिकार

आज के समानतावादी समाज में मानव और अल्पसंख्यकों के अधिकार को आधारभूत महत्व प्राप्त है जिसको संयुक्त राष्ट्र संघ की जनरल असेम्बली ने 10.12.1948 के अपने घोषणा पत्र में इस प्रकार प्रस्तुत किया है "सब मनुष्य स्वतंत्र पैदा होते हैं और उन्हें मानव अधिकार और आदर बराबरी के स्तर पर प्राप्त होते हैं। उनको चाहिए कि वह अपनी बुद्धि एवं आत्मा के अनुसार एक-दूसरे से भाई चारे का व्यवहार करें।" मानव-अधिकार की बराबरी का तात्पर्य यह है कि सभी मनुष्य कानून की दृष्टि में समान हैं। और उनको गुलामी, नाजायज़ गिरफ़्तारी एवं शोषण से आज़ादी मिलनी चाहिए। उन्हें वोट देने का अधिकार अपने धर्म, संस्कृति एवं भाषा, काम करने आने-जाने, बोलने लिखने-पढ़ने, स्वास्थ्य, शिक्षा, अच्छा जीवन स्तर के अधिकार समान स्तर के प्राप्त होंगे। इस घोषणा की पुष्टि 1966 में दो अंतर्राष्ट्रीय संविदाओं, शहरी एवं राजनीतिक अधिकारों पर अंतर्राष्ट्रीय प्रतिज्ञा (ICCPR) और आर्थिक, सामाजिक एवं सांस्कृतिक अधिकारों पर अंतर्राष्ट्रीय प्रतिज्ञा (ICESCR) की गयी। सभी मानव अधिकार हर मनुष्य को बिना धर्म, रंग, नस्ल, लिंग और भाषा के अंतर के दिये

गये और इसके लिये किसी प्रकार की राजनीतिक, राष्ट्रीय या सामाजिक या संपत्ति, जन्म, पद की कोई शर्त नहीं रखी गयी। अल्पसंख्यकों के लिये विशेष रूप से यह जमानत दी गयी कि उनको धर्म, विश्वास, भाषा, राय की स्वतंत्रता के साथ जान व माल की सुरक्षा अपनी सभ्यता व सामाजिक पहचान बनाये रखने, शैक्षिक संस्थाएँ खोलने और न्याय प्राप्त करने के अधिकार प्राप्त होंगे जो समानतावादी समाज का आवश्यक भाग होते हैं। इस बारे में महात्मा गांधी का कथन बड़ा महत्व रखता है—"किसी सभ्यता की अच्छाई बुराई का फैसला उसके अपने अल्पसंख्यकों के साथ बर्ताव से किया जा सकता है।"

सकारात्मक विशेष व्यवहार और समानता

अमानवीय व्यवहार अथवा जातीय व सामाजिक पक्षपात एवं दुर्व्यवहार को रोकने और उनसे उत्पन्न होने वाले दोषों को समाप्त करने के लिये इलाज के रूप में कुछ तरीकों को विशेष रूप से या अन्तर के बर्ताव को अपनाना पड़ता है, और क्योंकि इसका प्रयोग इलाज के तौर पर और असमानता को रोकने के लिये होता है इस कारण इसको सही और उचित बताया जाता है और इसको सकारात्मक प्रयास कहा जाता है।

संयुक्त राष्ट्र संघ के मानव अधिकार कौंसिल की सलाहकार समिति ने जाति, लिंग अथवा धर्म के आधार पर की जाने वाली ग़लत कार्यवाहियों के विरुद्ध इस तरीके पर कार्य करने का निर्देश दिया है ताकि प्रभावित व्यक्तियों या समूहों के दुख दूर किये जा सकें, उनको आवश्यक अधिकार बिना रोकटोक के मिलते रहें किन्तु इन प्रयासों को सामयिक रूप से जब तक आवश्यकता हो प्रयोग करना चाहिए क्योंकि यह कठोर कार्यवाही केवल विशेष परिस्थितियों में की जाती है और स्पष्ट रूप से समानता एवं मानव-मित्रता से मेल नहीं खाती। अंतरराष्ट्रीय कानून के विशेषज्ञ और राजनीतिक विद्वानों ने कहा है कि ये कार्यवाही समूहों की हानि की भरपाई और उनके मानवीय अधिकारों को बनाये रखने के लिये थोड़े समय के लिये करनी चाहिए जैसे भाषा, धर्म एवं शैक्षिक संस्थाओं की सुरक्षा व निर्माण अथवा पदों को सुरक्षित रखने के लिये यह कार्यवाही उचित एवं सीमित स्तर पर होना चाहिए। ये स्पष्टीकरण संयुक्त राष्ट्र संघ की धारा 8 और 14 में किया गया है। जैसे महिलाओं के

साथ भेद-भाव समाप्त करने के लिये और अल्पसंख्यकों को अवसर प्रदान करने के लिये ऐसी कार्यवाही उस समय तक करना चाहिए जब तक ये उद्देश्य पूरा न हो जाये। हमारे देश में ICESCR के अंतर्राष्ट्रीय समझौते की धारा 2 में यह स्पष्टीकरण करने की सलाह दी गई कि किसी भी पिछड़े वर्ग को आगे बढ़ने एवं दूसरों के बराबर उन्नति करने के प्रयासों को समानता या न्याय के विरुद्ध न समझा जाये। "इस कारण इस प्रस्ताव को मानव अधिकार कमेटी ने दूसरे अंतर्राष्ट्रीय समझौते की धारा 26 के अंतर्गत ये बात सम्मिलित करलीं कि कभी-कभी समानता के नियमों के विरुद्ध किसी पिछड़े हुए वर्ग या समूह को उनके उचित अधिकार दिलवाने के लिये राज्य को सकारात्मक प्रयास, एक विशेष समय के लिये करने पड़ते हैं। उनको समानता या न्याय के विरुद्ध न समझा जाये। यह प्रयत्न कानूनी, अदालती या प्रबंध संबंधी हो सकते हैं जो किसी अल्पसंख्यक के धर्म, भाषा एवं संस्कृति की सुरक्षा के लिये किए जाते हैं और उनको अनुचित नहीं ठहराया जा सकता है।

अंतर्राष्ट्रीय अदालत ने भी अपने कुछ फैसलों में विशेषकर दक्षिण पश्चिमी अफ्रीका के मुद्दमों में इस नियम को माना है कि कानून की दृष्टि में समानता की मांग है कि जो लोग कमजोर और पिछड़ गये हैं उनके साथ विशेष बर्ताव किया जाये।

महिला, पुरुष की समानता की समस्या

समानतावादी समाज की नींव स्त्री एवं पुरुष की समानता पर रखी गयी है। इसमें स्त्रियों को सामाजिक, राजनीतिक एवं कानूनी स्तर पर पुरुषों के बराबर अधिकार दिए गए हैं और उन्हें गृहहिंसा, लिंगभेद, छेड़छाड़, बुरा बर्ताव, निकाह और तलाक़ में अधिकता के विरुद्ध सुरक्षा दी गई है और पुरुषों के बराबर अधिकार दिए गए हैं। महिलाओं का प्रतिनिधित्व देश के विभिन्न भागों में दिखाई दे रहा है। अतः इस समय भारत के राष्ट्रपति, स्पीकर, कानून, अदालत, प्रशासन और प्राइवेट सेक्टर के उच्च पदों पर महिलाएँ नियुक्त हैं और उनकी शिक्षा की ओर विशेष ध्यान दिया जा रहा है। विश्व के विभिन्न देशों में महिलाओं के साथ प्राचीन समय से अन्याय एवं असमानता का व्यवहार किया जाता था, उनको वोट देने का अधिकार, पैतृक संपत्ति में अधिकार, पदों और नौकरियों में

स्थान नहीं दिया जाता था। उनकी चर्चा तुच्छ स्वर में पुस्तकों, समाचार पत्रों, कहावतों यहां तक कि धार्मिक व्याख्याओं में की जाती थी। इसके विरुद्ध पूरे विश्व में विरोध प्रकट किया गया और महिलाओं को बराबर का अधिकार देने के लिये आंदोलन चलाये गये। रोमन युग में महिलाओं का क्रय-विक्रय आम था। मसीही कलेसा में महिलाओं को तुच्छ एवं जन्म से दोषी माना जाता था। प्राचीन भारत में और इस्लाम से पहले अरब में लड़कियों को जीवित गाड़ दिया जाता था। चीन, जापान, इटली, स्पेन में महिलाओं को मारने पीटने की प्रथा प्रचलित थी। और उनके विरुद्ध भाँति-भाँति की दिल तोड़ने वाली कहावतें और मुहावरे प्रयोग किये जाते थे। मनुस्मृति, भगवतगीता और महाभारत में महिलाओं की गणना, विकलांग, पिछड़े और नाकारा वर्ग में की जाती थी, विधवा और बांझ महिलाओं का जीवन बड़ा कठिन था किन्तु अब हालात बिल्कुल बदल चुके हैं और महिलाओं के साथ आदर और न्यायपूर्ण व्यवहार किया जाता है।

कानूनी एवं राजनीतिक समानता

क़ानूनी समानता अर्थात कानून की दृष्टि में सब मनुष्यों के बराबर होने का दृष्टिकोंण, बड़े संघर्ष और कठिनाइयों के बाद विश्व में विस्थापित हुआ। प्राचीन समय में इसकी कल्पना भी नहीं की जा सकती थी। प्राचीन भारत में मनुस्मृति एवं हिन्दु कानून जाति के आधार पर खुलकर मनुष्यों में अंतर करता था और हर विषय में उच्चवर्ग (ब्राह्मण, क्षत्रिय इत्यादि) के लोगों को महत्व दिया जाता था। शूद्रों के साथ अवनयाय एवं क्रूरता का व्यवहार किया जाता था। यूनान, मिस्र और यूरोप में दास और दासियों को मनुष्य नहीं समझा जाता था। कानून निर्माण, प्रबंधन, व्यवसाय शिक्षा इत्यादि जीवन के हर क्षेत्र में ऊँच-नीच एवं असमानता फैली हुई थी। राजनीतिक अधिकार कुछ लोगों, परिवारों अथवा समूहों को प्राप्त थे किन्तु अब हालात पूरे तौर पर बदल चुके हैं। हर तरफ कानूनी समानता एवं राजनीतिक समानता पर जोर दिया जा रहा है।

मानव अधिकारों की सुरक्षा और उनका लाभ प्रत्येक व्यक्ति तक पहुँचाने का उचित प्रबंध हर स्तर पर उपलब्ध है विश्व की तमाम महिलाओं एवं पुरुषों के लिये कानून, लिंग, धर्म, समाज, राजनीति, आर्थिक, शैक्षिक एवं सांस्कृतिक स्तर पर पूर्ण समानता का दृष्टिकोण स्वीकार्य है। इस संदर्भ में विश्व के बड़े

धार्मिक, राजनीतिक एवं कानूनी चिंतकों ने बहुत कार्य किया है किन्तु फिर भी समानतावादी समाज को संपूर्ण संसार में सक्रिय बनाने की आवश्यकता है।

URDU

باب اول

سیکولرازم ۔ ہندوستان میں کامیاب تجربہ

پروفیسر مرزا امر بیگ

سماجیات کے عالموں، جن میں میکس ویبر سے لے کر پیٹر برگر تک شامل ہیں، کا خیال ہے کہ سیکولرازم یا نامذہبیت موجودہ زمانہ کا ایک پائیدار اور خوشگوار تحفہ ہے جو بیک وقت شہری زندگی کی سہولتوں، عقلیت پسندی، پیشہ وارنہ مہارت، چاق وچوبند انتظامیہ کا مجموعہ پیش کرتا ہے جس میں کسی بھی مذہبی عقیدہ یا رسم ورواج کو ختم کرنے کی گنجائش نہیں ہوتی۔ نامذہبیت کا تصور دنیا میں 1648 میں پیدا ہوا جب مسیحی کلیسا کا اختیار واقتدار بادشاہوں کی طرف منتقل ہوگیا اور فرانس، انگلستان اور یورپ کے دوسرے ملکوں میں مذہبی معاملات میں قوم کو فیصلہ کرنے کا حق دیا گیا اور سیکولر انداز فکر کو ترقی کی علامت قرار دیا گیا۔ یہاں یہ بات صاف کردینا ضروری ہے کہ سیکولر لفظ کے معنی وتشریح مختلف ملکوں میں پائے جانے والے تاریخی وتہذیبی حالات کے مطابق الگ الگ بیان کئے گئے ہیں۔ مثلاً امریکہ اور ہندوستان میں اسکا مفہوم ایک دوسرے سے مختلف اور جداگانہ ہے۔ ہندوستان میں سیکولرازم کا مطلب یہ ہے کہ مملکت یا ریاست کسی مذہب کی مخالف یا معتقد نہیں اور اسکے نامذہبی ہونے کا سب سے بڑا

ثبوت یہ ہے کہ یہاں ہر مذہب کے پیروؤں کو مذہبی آزادی اور برابری حاصل ہے۔ مغربی ممالک میں یہ لفظ مذہب کے مخالف معنی رکھتا ہے یعنی سیکولر سے مراد مذہب مخالف رجحان لیا جاتا ہے۔ اور اسکی بنیاد ان تاریخی واقعات پر ہے جن کی وجہ سے کلیسا اور مملکت (بادشاہوں) میں تصادم کی نوبت آئی اور مملکت نے چرچ اور مذہبی اداروں کو سماجی برتری اور اقتدار سے بے دخل کر دیا اور اسکے خلاف منظّم اور منفی رویہ اختیار کیا۔ اس کی ایک حد تک ذمہ داری مذہبی حلقوں کی تنگ نظری اور سخت گیری پر بھی ہے۔ لیکن خوش قسمتی سے ہندوستان میں ایسا نہیں ہوا۔ یہاں کے دستور میں یہ صاف طور پر اعلان کیا گیا کہ جمہوریہ ہند کا کوئی سرکاری مذہب نہیں ہے۔ اور وہ ہر مذہب کے ساتھ انصاف و برابری کا سلوک کرے گی اور اس ملک کے شہریوں کو عقیدہ وضمیر کی پوری آزادی ہوگی۔ اس لیے اسے یاد رکھنا ضروری ہے کہ ہندوستان میں سیکولرازم کا تصور آیا تو مغرب سے مگر اس کا مفہوم اور مطلب وہاں سے بالکل الگ اور مختلف ہے۔ اب امریکہ کے دستور کی پہلی ترمیم کو دیکھئے جس میں کہا گیا ہے کہ ''امریکہ کی کانگریس (پارلیمنٹ) کسی مذہب کی تشکیل یا اسکو اختیار کرنے کے خلاف کوئی قانون نہیں بنائے گی''۔ امریکی صدر جیفرسن نے اس کی وضاحت کرتے ہوئے کہا تھا کہ ''ہمارے دستور نے کلیسا اور مملکت کے درمیان ایک واضح حد فاصل بنا دی ہے''۔ اسی طرح کی باتیں آسٹریلیا کے دستور میں بھی کہی گئی ہیں کہ مذہب کے موافق یا مخالف نہ تو کوئی قانون بنایا جائے گا اور نہ کسی قسم کا مذہبی معیار یا امتحان عام ملازمتوں کے لئے رکھا جائے گا۔

ہندوستانی سیکورازم کامفہوم اوراسکی خصوصیات

ہندوستانی دستور جو 26 جنوری 1950 کو ہمارے ملک میں نافذ ہوا اس میں سیکولرازم کی تشریح یوں کی گئی ہے۔

۱۔ مملکت یا ریاست کا کوئی مذہب نہیں ہوگا۔

۲۔ سرکاری آمدنی کوکسی مذہب کے فروغ دینے میں صرف نہیں کیا جائے گا۔

۳۔ ریاست کے لئے ضروری ہوگا کہ وہ دفعہ 25 کے تحت دیئے گئے مذہبی آزادی کے حقوق کے متعلق اور مالی یا معاشی یا تہذیبی امور کے متعلق نا مذہبی رویہ اپنائے اوراس پرعمل کرے۔

۴۔ چھوت چھات کو آئینی طور پر ناجائز اور ایک جرم قرار دیا گیا ہے۔ (دفعہ 17)۔

۵۔ آئین کی دفعہ 25 کے تحت ہر شہری کوحق ہوگا کہ وہ جس مذہب یا عقیدہ کو چاہے اختیار کرے لیکن عام نظم ونسق، اخلاق اورصحت عامہ کے تقاضوں کے پیش نظر ان حقوق پر ریاست قانونی پابندیاں لگاسکتی ہے۔اسی کے ساتھ یہ حقوق آئین میں عطا کئے گئے بنیادی حقوق کے ماتحت ہونگے۔

۶۔ ملک کی عدالتیں خصوصاً سپریم کورٹ اس بارے میں ریاستی احکامات پرآئین کی تشریحات میں احتساب کرتی رہے گی۔ 1973 میں کیشونند بھارتی کے خلاف ریاست کیرالا کے مقدمہ میں سپریم کورٹ نے اپنے فیصلہ میں یہ وضاحت کی کہ ہندوستانی

آئین کے اجزاء ترکیبی میں سیکولرازم ایک بنیادی اور اہم جزو ہے اور اسکی تائید میں 1975 میں اندرا گاندھی بمقابلہ راج نرائن کے مقدمہ میں سپریم کورٹ نے اپنا ایک اور فیصلہ سنایا۔

مگر ہمارے ملک میں مملکت اور مذہبی اداروں کے درمیان کوئی حد فاصل یا مخالفت نہیں پائے جاتی۔ ہمارے آئین کی دفعہ 16 (5) مذہبی اداروں کے نظم ونسق کے لئے ضابطے بنانے کی اجازت شہریوں کو دیتی ہے۔ اسی طرح عقیدہ اور مذہبی حقوق کی آزادی دفعات 25 اور 26 کے تحت ہر شہری کو دی گئی ہے۔ البتہ ریاست کو عام نظم و نسق، اخلاق اور صحت عامہ کے تقاضوں کے پیش نظر اور بنیادی حقوق کے تحفظ کی خاطر ان پر قانونی پابندیاں لگانے کا اختیار رہوگا جسکی جانچ ملکی عدالتیں خاص کر سپریم کورٹ کرتی رہے گی۔

چنانچہ کوئی بھی ہندوستانی شہری یا ادارہ مذہبی یا امور خیر سے تعلق رکھنے والے ادارے قائم کرسکتا ہے اور ملکی قانون کے تحت اس کے لئے جائداد منقولہ وغیر منقولہ کی خرید فروخت کرسکتا ہے اور ان کا انتظام کرسکتا ہے۔ اس میں تعلیمی ادارے بھی شامل ہیں، اور اس سہولت کا دروازہ صرف اقلیتوں کے لئے ہی نہیں بلکہ سماج کے ہر طبقہ وفرقہ کے لئے شہریوں کے قائم کئے ہوئے تعلیمی اداروں میں کھلا ہوا ہے۔

اگر تعلیمی اداروں میں مذہبی امور یا دینیات کی تعلیم دی جاتی ہے تو ہمارا آئین اسے سیکولرازم کے خلاف نہیں مانتا۔ اسکا کہنا یہ ہے کی بغیر شناخت کھوئے ہمارے ملک میں سب مذہبوں کی تعلیم دی جاسکتی ہے بشرطیکہ وہ ملکی قوانین وضوابط کے اندر ہو۔

اس طرح ریاست سرکاری آمدنی (جسکا بیشتر حصہ ٹیکسوں کی شکل میں شہریوں سے حاصل ہوتا ہے۔) کا کچھ حصہ مذہبی ادارہ یا کسی مذہبی تقریب کے لئے دفعہ 27 کے تحت دے سکتی ہے جیسے تامل ناڈو اور کیرالا کی ریاستی حکومیتں کچھ ہندو مندروں کی مدد کے لئے روپیہ دیتی ہیں، جنہیں آزادی سے قبل ہندوستان کی کچھ ریاستوں کے راجہ مدد دیا کرتے تھے۔ جبکہ امریکن سپریم کورٹ نے ایک فیصلہ میں یہ کہا کہ رومن کیتھولک اسکول تک جانے کے مصارف بچوں کو ریاست دینے کی مجاز نہیں۔ ہاں یہ بات ضرور ہے کہ سرکاری تعلیمی اداروں میں جن کا سارا خرچ ریاست برداشت کرتی ہے، کسی مذہب کی تعلیم دفعہ 28 الف کے تحت نہیں دی جا سکتی لیکن جو ادارے کسی ٹرسٹ یا وقف یا شہریوں نے قایم کئے ہیں اور وہاں کسی خاص مذہب کی تعلیمات دی جاتی ہیں تو ان کو سرکار مالی امداد دے سکتی ہے اور ان کے وجود کو تسلیم کر سکتی ہے۔

ان باتوں سے ظاہر ہوتا ہے کہ ہندوستانی دستور امریکن دستور کی طرح مذہبی اداروں سے مملکت کا بالکل بے تعلق رہنا یا ان سے بالکل الگ تھلگ رہنا پسند نہیں کرتا۔ بلکہ وہ مملکت کو ترغیب دیتا ہے کہ صحیح نامذہبیت کے تحت وہ سب مذہبوں سے یکساں برابری کا سلوک کرے۔

ہندوستان میں سیکولرازم کا تجربہ کامیاب رہا ہے اور اس سے قومی یکجہتی اور بھائی چارہ کو بڑی تقویت پہنچی ہے، مگر اسی کے ساتھ ہی یہ بھی حقیقت ہے کہ بعض سیاسی، مذہبی مفکرین اور اس سے بھی بڑھ کر دلچسپ بات یہ ہے کہ کچھ قدامت پسند مذہبی طبقوں اور آزاد خیال طبقوں دونوں کی طرف سے سیکولرازم کی مخالفت یہ کہہ کر کی جارہی ہے کہ

وہ ماڈرن ازم اور ترقی کے راستہ میں روڑہ اٹکا رہا ہے۔ اسی طرح ایک قسم کی تہذیبی جنگ سیکولرازم کے حامیوں اور مخالفوں میں ہو رہی ہے جس میں دانشور، صحافی، مذہبی عالم، عدالتیں، میڈیا سب ہی شامل ہیں۔ دنیا میں آزادی پسماندگی، انتہا پسندی اور حق پسندی کے درمیان یہ آویزش نئی نہیں ہے، دیکھنا یہ ہے کہ جیت کس کی ہوتی ہے۔ مذہبی حلقے، جارحانہ سیکولرازم جو زندگی کے ہر شعبہ پر حاوی ہونا چاہتا ہے، کے سخت مخالف ہیں، کیونکہ وہ عوامی زندگی سے مذہب کو بالکل بے دخل کرنا ضروری سمجھتے ہیں۔ دوسری طرف سیکولرازم کے کٹر پرستار یہ سمجھتے ہیں کہ مذہب کے عمل دخل سے حریت پسندی، تحقیق اور ترقی میں رکاوٹ پڑتی ہے۔ انصاف کی بات یہ ہے کہ دونوں فریق غلو کا شکار ہیں اور اعتدال سے کام نہیں لیتے۔

باب دوم:

قومی یکجہتی

ڈاکٹر آر ایس وارشنے

قومی یکجہتی یا ایکتا ایک بڑا وسیع لفظ ہے اور اسکے معنی، مفہوم، شکل، اجزاء اور ترقی کو سمجھنے کے لئے ضروری ہے کہ اسکے تین ضروری پہلوؤں پر پورے طور سے نظر ڈالی جائے۔

ا۔ سب سے پہلے ہم کو قومی یکجہتی کے تصور اور اس سے جڑے ہوئے مسئلوں کے بارے میں سماجی علوم کے ماہرین اور سماجی کارکنوں کے خیالات واحساسات کو جاننا چاہیے۔

۲۔ دوسرے نمبر پر ان واقعات، حالات، تاریخی وسماجی پس منظر کو دیکھنا چاہیے۔ جس کا سامنا ہمارے ملک اور وہاں کے رہنے والوں نے کیا ہے۔ یہ ایک ایسا ملا جلا منظر ہے جس میں قومی بھائی چارے کے ساتھ آپس کے لڑائی جھگڑوں، تعصب اور غیر انسانی برتاؤ کی تصویریں نظر آتی ہیں، جنہوں نے ہمارے ملک کو ترقی و طاقت کے راستے سے ہٹا کر کمزور اور بدنام کیا ہے۔

۳۔ تیسرے مرحلہ پر ہمیں ان کوششوں اور اقدامات کا مطالعہ کرنا چاہیے جو حالات کو

سدھارنے اور قومی ایکتا کو بڑھانے کے لئے کئے گئے اور تحریر، تقریر اور انفرادی و اجتماعی کوششوں کا جائزہ لینا چاہیے کہ اس مقصد کے حصول میں کہاں تک کامیابی مل پائی۔

قومی ایکتا کا دائرہ بڑا پھیلا ہوا ہے۔ سماجی ترقی، وطن کی محبت، قومی ورثہ، اہم تاریخی واقعات اور ہمارے وطنی بھائیوں کے شاندار کارناموں نے اسے بڑھایا اور زندگی کے ہر شعبہ پر اثر ڈالا ہے۔ یہ ہمارا فرض ہے کہ ہر قیمت پر اسکی حفاظت کریں اور اسکی اہمیت کو پوری طرح سمجھیں۔

قومی ایکتا کے نظریہ کا مفہوم، اسکے مختلف مثبت پہلو، اور منفی اثرات

اس نظریہ کی بنیاد وطن پروری، انسانیت دوستی، اخلاق، رواداری اور مختلف دائروں میں کئے گئے اچھے کاموں اور ڈسپلن پر ہے۔ اگر ہمارے ملک میں قومی اور سماجی سطح پر ترقی، رواداری، درگزر، اچھی باتوں کے سیکھنے، مل جل کر رہنے اور صبر وضبط کے جذبات واحساسات پیدا ہو جائیں اور سب شہری اس پر عمل کرنے لگیں تو یقیناً ہم کو ایکتا اور بھائی چارہ کی نعمت حاصل ہو جائے گی۔ اور اسکے برعکس اگر ایک دوسرے سے نفرت، حسد، توڑ پھوڑ، الگ رہنے، نفاق اور اتحاد و اتفاق سے دور بھاگنے اور مذہب، زبان اور تہذیب کے معاملات میں کٹرپن اور تعصب کا رویہ اپنایا جائے گا تو قومی اتحاد پارہ پارہ ہو جائے گا اور ملک تباہی کے راستہ پر آ جائے گا۔

بھائی چارے کے لئے ضروری ہے کہ ہم اپنے سماجی اور ملک میں سیاسی طور پر اچھی حکومت اور سمجھ دار قیادت قائم کریں اور علم تاریخ وسماجیات کی روشنی میں ملک سے

وفاداری اوراپنے ہم وطنوں سے اشتراک کریں، قانون کا احترام کریں، مذہب کی سچی تعلیمات پر عمل کریں، دینیات، فلسفہ اورعوامی سطح پر تعلیم کے انتظام اور میڈیا کے مثبت اورعملی اثرات سے عام لوگوں کو فائدہ پہنچائیں تاکہ وہ قومی اتحاد اور ملک کے شاندارتہذیبی، علمی اورتاریخی ورثہ کی قدر کرسکیں۔ اس سلسلہ میں نفسیاتی طور پر نسل، مذہب، زبان، رسم ورواج اور ذات پات اورعلاقائی خصوصیات بڑی اہمیت رکھتی ہیں بشرطیکہ ان کوصحیح اور مثبت طور پر لوگوں کے سامنے پیش کیا جائے۔ ورنہ نسل، مذہب، ذات پات، زبان، خاندان، قبیلہ اورعلاقوں کوکٹر پن تعصب اورنفرت بڑھانے کے لئے آسانی سے استعمال کیا جاسکتا ہے اور ہمارے ملک میں اسکی افسوسناک مثالیں بھی موجود ہیں۔ یہ کام ہمارے سیاسی اور مذہبی لیڈر، پارٹیاں، انتظامیہ، سماجی کارکن، تجارت، تعلیم، ملازمت، زراعت اورمختلف پیشوں اورکاموں میں لگے افراد اور ادارے سب ہی کرسکتے ہیں۔ میڈیا، پارلیمنٹ، مندر، مسجد، گرجا گھر، گوردوارہ، فوج، پولیس اورسب سے بڑھ کرسمجھ دار رائے عامہ کٹرپن، بداخلاقی اورخودغرضی اور ملک دشمنی کےمنفی اورمضراثرات کودورکرسکتے ہیں۔

ہمارے ملک کے لوگ اپنے مذہب، زبان، رسم ورواج اور وطن سے محبت کرتے ہیں۔ یہ قومی یکجہتی کے لئے فال نیک ہے اوراس کی مدد سے ایکتا اور بھائی چارے کو بڑھایا جاسکتا ہے۔ اسی کے ساتھ ہی یہ بھی ضروری ہے کہ ہمارا سماج مذہبی، تمدنی، سیاسی اور انسانی رجحانات پرغورکرے اور ڈکٹیٹرشپ، تعصب، علیحدگی اور اختلاف کی طاقتوں کو بڑھنے اور پھیلنے سے روکے۔

یہاں یہ سوال پیدا ہوتا ہے کہ قومی یکجہتی کیا چیز ہے؟ وہ کس کے لئے ہے اور اسے کیسے قائم کیا اور پھیلایا جاسکتا ہے؟ قومی یکجہتی ایک ایسا جذبہ اور طاقت ہے جو ہمارے ملک اور سماج کے مختلف اجزاء کو اختلاف میں اشتراک کے بنیادی اصول کے تحت جوڑے رکھتی ہے اور وطن کی محبت اور وفاداری کو بڑھاتی ہے۔ یہ ہمارے ملک، یہاں کے رہنے والوں، یہاں کی تہذیب و تاریخ اور اخلاقی قدردں کا اٹوٹ حصہ ہے۔ جوسب کے لئے مفیداور ضروری ہے اور اسکومختلف اداروں اور تنظیموں کے ذریعہ محفوظ رکھا جاسکتا ہے۔

پہلے یہ سمجھ لینا چاہیے کہ ''قوم'' کیا مفہوم یا معنی رکھتی ہے۔ بدقسمتی سے سیاست کے عالموں، مؤرخوں اور سماجیات کے ماہرین نے اسکے الگ الگ معنی بیان کئے ہیں، جس کی وجہ سے اسے سمجھنے میں دشواری ہوتی ہے۔ کہیں سیاسی برتری، کہیں مذہبی تفوق یا کسی نسل یا زبان کی بنا پر قوم کے ایسے معنی اور مفہوم پہنائے گئے ہیں جن کی وجہ سے وہ اصلیت سے دور ہوگئے۔ قوم بہت سے اجزاء اور مرحلوں کا مرکب ہے مثلاً دستور سازی، سیکولرازم، اپنی حکومت، مرکزیت وغیرہ۔ لیگ آف نیشنس نے قوم کی تعریف یہ کی تھی کہ ''اس میں وہ تمام مملکتیں شامل ہیں جو آزاد ہوں اور بلالحاظ طرز حکومت یا سماجی ترقی اقتدار اعلیٰ کی مالک ہوں''۔ بہرحال قومیت کا تصور، سیاسی اتحاد، آزاد حکومت کے قیام اور اقتدار اعلیٰ کو ظاہر کرتا ہے۔

''قوم'' اور ''مملکت'' کے درمیان فرق کرنا مشکل ہے کیونکہ دانشوروں نے

اس بارے میں کوئی صاف بات نہیں کہی ۔ کہیں دونوں کو ایک کہا گیا ہے، کہیں الگ الگ شناخت کی گئی ہے، اور گول مول الفاظ میں دونوں لفظوں کو استعمال کیا گیا ہے ۔ اصل واقعہ یہ ہے کہ قوم '' مملکت '' سے وسیع مفہوم رکھتی ہے ۔ وہ مختلف طبقوں کی آبادی پر مشتمل ہوتی ہے جو کسی جغرافیائی خطّہ میں آباد ہوتی ہے اور مختلف قسم کے کام کرتی ہے ۔ انتظام اور قانون کی بالادستی کے لئے اسی کے تحت ایک ادارہ '' مملکت '' ہوتا ہے جو قوم کی شناخت کے لئے طاقت کا سرچشمہ ہوتا ہے ۔ جو لوگ یہ کہتے ہیں کہ قوم کے لئے مملکت کا ہونا لازمی نہیں وہ غلطی پر ہیں ۔ قوم کسی علاقہ میں آباد ان لوگوں کو کہتے ہیں جو اپنے او پر حکومت کرنے کے لئے مملکت کو قائم کرتے ہیں ۔ جو اس علاقہ میں امن دامان اور زندگی کی سہولتوں کو فراہم کرتی ہے ۔ قوم کی شناخت، اور تشکیل میں نسل، مذہب، زبان، تاریخ اور سب سے بڑھ کر لوگوں کی مرضی یا رائے عامہ کا بڑا دخل ہوتا ہے ۔ جو ایک سماجی کارکن ہونے کے ساتھ ساتھ اپنے کو ایک قوم بنانے کی تحریک چلاتے ہیں اور اپنے او پر حکومت کرنے کے لئے مملکت کو قائم کرتے ہیں ۔ اس طرح سے ہم سماج، قوم اور مملکت کی الگ الگ حیثیتوں کو اور ان کی اہمیت کو سمجھ سکتے ہیں ۔ قوم کے لئے ضروری ہے کہ اس کا ایک مخصوص متعین جغرافیائی علاقہ (ملک) ہو، اسکے پاس انتظام کے لئے لوگوں کی مرضی کے مطابق ایک مملکت ہو، اسکی تاریخی وتمدنی خصوصیات ہوں، قانون کی بالادستی اور تہذیب واخلاق کی قدریں موجود ہوں اور وہاں کے رہنے والوں میں اتحاد اور اتفاق پایا جائے ۔ اسکی ایک مشترک زبان ہو، ایک قومی جھنڈا ہو، ایک قومی ترانہ

ہو، معاشی وسائل ہوں اور نفسیاتی و جذباتی طور پر وطن سے وفاداری اور کچھ ایسے قومی مقاصد و معیار ہوں جن سے دنیا میں اسکی پہچان ہو سکے۔ ان ساری باتوں میں تاریخی و سیاسی عوامل کی بنا پر برابر ترقی و تبدیلی ہوتی رہتی ہے۔ قوم کے اندر مختلف اور ایک سے زائد سماج ہو سکتے ہیں جن کی بنیاد رسم و رواج، روایات اور طریقہ زندگی پر ہوتی ہے۔

یہ بھی یاد رکھنا چاہیے کہ قومیت کا احساس اور تحفظ نہایت ضروری ہے ورنہ اسکا انجام خانہ جنگی خون خرابہ، غلامی اور زوال ہوتا ہے۔ اسی لئے ہم سب کو اپنے ملک کی سالمیت، آزادی، جھنڈے، زبان، قومی ورثہ اور خصوصیات کا احترام کرنا چاہیے اور ان سب کا وفادار رہنا چاہیے۔

جو لوگ ایسا نہیں کرتے اور ان خطوط پر نہیں سوچتے وہ دیش سے دشمنی کرتے ہیں، اور ان سے ملک و قوم کو تباہی اور بربادی کا خطرہ لاحق رہتا ہے۔

اقتدار اعلیٰ اور آزادی کے ساتھ یہ بھی عوام کی ذمہ داری ہے کہ وہ اسکی حفاظت کریں یعنی برسر اقتدار حکومت یا کوئی فرد یا گروہ اگر بدعنوانی، رشوت ستانی یا ملک دشمن کام کرے تو جدوجہد کر کے (جس میں احتجاج کے ساتھ مظاہرے اور بائیکاٹ وغیرہ بھی شامل ہے) ایسی حکومت کو ہٹا دیں یا ہٹنے پر مجبور کر دیں اور ایسے لوگوں کو سخت سزا دلوائیں۔

قومی ایکتا کے لئے یہ بھی ضروری ہے کہ سماج اور اس میں شامل تمام طبقے اور ادارے ملک کے سیاسی، تہذیبی اور سماجی اتحاد کو باقی رکھیں، اسکا مطلب یہ نہیں کہ وہ

سب ایک میں ضم ہو جائیں اور اپنا علیحدہ وجود بالکل ختم کرلیں۔ ان کو چاہیے کہ وہ اپنی سرگرمیوں کو قومی اتحاد اور بہتری کے تحت کریں اور مل جل کر ایک دوسرے سے رواداری برتیں، ان کے جذبات کا خیال رکھیں۔ مشترک تہذیب وتمدن بڑا اچھا تحفہ ہے جس پر ہندوستان کو فخر ہے۔

قومی ایکتا کا تقاضہ ہے کہ ہم اپنے لسانی، مذہبی، سماجی اختلافات کو قومی تانے بانے میں جگہ دیں۔ یہ کام تھوڑے صبر وتحمل اور برداشت سے ہوسکتا ہے۔ قومی اتحاد ان اختلافات کے باوجود قائم رکھا جاسکتا ہے۔ جس کا ثبوت ہماری تاریخ اور معاشرتی زندگی، خواہ وہ گاؤں میں ہو یا شہر میں، دے رہی ہے۔ ہم کو ٹکراؤ اور احساس برتری سے بچنا چاہیے۔ منظّم طریقہ پر سب کو یہ کوشش کرنا چاہیے کہ اپنی مخصوص روایات اور طریقہ زندگی کو قومی دھارے میں سمو دیا جائے اور نفرت و دوری کو مٹایا جائے۔ یہ کام مشکل ضرور ہے لیکن ناممکن نہیں۔

آزادی کے بعد ہمارے ملک اور سماج میں اس سلسلہ میں بہت کام ہوا ہے، اچھا بھی اور برا بھی۔ یہ مسئلہ بڑا اہم ہے۔ ایک طرف ہمارے لیڈروں، میڈیا، مذہبی اور سماجی کارکنوں نے قومی یکجہتی اور بھائی چارے کے لئے زبردست کوششیں کیں، قربانیاں دیں اور اس ضروری فرض کی طرف ملک والوں کو متوجہ کیا۔ مگر اسی کے ساتھ بدقسمتی سے کچھ لوگوں نے جن میں سیاسی پارٹیاں، لیڈر، مذہبی اور سماجی جماعتیں، میڈیا اور تعلیم یافتہ لوگ شامل تھے اختلاف اور نفرت کے جذبات کو بھڑکایا اور پھیلایا۔

زبان، مذہب، علاقہ، رسم ورواج، ذات پات اور سیاسی امور کو لے کر فرقہ وارانہ فسادات، لوٹ مار، تباہی اور بربادی کے ایسے واقعات پیش آئے جن سے ہندوستان کی بڑی بدنامی ہوئی اور ترقی کی دوڑ میں ہم پیچھے رہ گئے۔ یہ یاد رکھنا چاہیے کہ ہم نے آزادی بڑی مشکل سے، اچھی خاصی قیمت اور قربانی دے کر حاصل کی ہے۔ ہندوستان جیسے بڑے ملک میں جہاں مختلف اور متعدد زبانیں، مذہب، رسم ورواج پائے جاتے ہیں۔ یکجہتی اور سب کو ایک ساتھ جوڑنے کا کام آسان نہیں تھا۔ ہندوستان کی آزاد حکومت نے اس کٹھن مسئلہ کو حل کرنے کے لئے مختلف قدم اٹھائے۔ یکجہتی لانے کے لئے اعلیٰ قسم کا دستور بنایا گیا۔ وسائل کو ترقی کے لئے برسرکار لانے کے لئے عمدہ منصوبے تیار کئے گئے، تقسیم ہند اور تعلیمی، سماجی و معاشی پسماندگی دور کرنے کے لئے مؤثر پروگرام بنائے گئے۔ اس راستہ میں بڑی رکاوٹیں پیش آئیں۔ ملک کی تباہ ہوئی معیشت اور بگڑی ہوئی اخلاقی و معاشرتی حالت کو سدھارنا آسان کام نہیں تھا، پھر سے بسانے، قومی کردار اور یکجہتی کی تشکیل میں نابرابری، مفلسی، جہالت اور تنگ نظری کی وجہ سے بڑی دقتیں پیش آئیں۔ بہرحال ان کوششوں کا اچھا نتیجہ نکلا اور ملک کی سماجی و معاشی زندگی میں خاصی تبدیلی آئی مگر اب بھی مسئلے پورے طور پر حل نہیں ہوئے۔ ابھی اور کام اور توجہ کی ضرورت ہے جس میں سب شہریوں کو حصہ لینا چاہیے۔

قومی یکجہتی کے راستہ میں بڑی رکاوٹیں حسب ذیل ہیں

ا۔ ملک میں کچھ ایسے طبقے، افراد اور ادارے موجود ہیں جو اپنے مخصوص تہذیبی ورثہ خاص کر مذہب، زبان، ریت رواج کی آڑ لے کر قومی ایکتا اور بھائی چارے کے خلاف ہیں اور ناانصافی اور تشدد کے راستہ پر چل رہے ہیں۔ یہ لوگ اپنی برتری ظاہر کر کے ملک کو اپنی مرضی کے مطابق غلط راستہ پر لے جانا چاہتے ہیں۔

۲۔ قومی ایکتا کے مخالف تعصب اور تنگ نظری سے کام لے کر جمہوریت اور سیکولرازم کے خلاف زبردست تحریک چلا رہے ہیں۔ تاریخی واقعات کو توڑ موڑ کر، بے بنیاد الزامات لگا کر ہمارے شاندار ماضی کو بدنام کر رہے ہیں۔ مثلاً کچھ انتہا پسند ہندو مسلمانوں کو غیر ملکی، ظالم ٹھہراتے ہیں اور مسلمان بادشاہوں کے ظلم وستم کی داستانیں مبالغہ کے ساتھ سنا کر عوام میں جوش پھیلاتے اور گمراہ کرتے ہیں۔ وہ ایک مخصوص کلچر اور طریقہ حکومت (ہندوتا) ملک پر تھوپنا چاہتے ہیں۔ دوسری طرف بعض شدت پسند مسلمان افراد اور پارٹیاں ہندوؤں کے مذہب، تاریخ اور رسم و رواج کو طرح طرح سے بدنام کرنے کی کوشش کرتے ہیں اور ان کے ساتھ تعاون کرنے کو برا کہتے ہیں۔ بدقسمتی سے دانش وروں اور میڈیا کا ایک طبقہ ان ملک دشمن خیالات کی تائید منظّم طریقہ پر کر رہا ہے۔

۳۔ ایک اور افسوسناک رجحان ملک میں بعض موہوم خطرات اور مبالغہ آمیز اندیشوں کے بنا پر فرقہ وارانہ منافرت اور علیحدگی پسندی کو ہوا دے رہا ہے مثلاً بعض لیڈر، پارٹیاں، ادارے اور اخباران باتوں کو اچھالتے ہیں کہ ملک میں تبدیلی مذہب کا بڑا

زور ہے، مخصوص مذہب یا فرقہ کی آبادی میں زبردست اضافہ ہورہا ہے، یا نفرت اور دشمنی کی بنا پر فرقہ وارانہ قتل و غارت اور تباہی کا اندیشہ ہر وقت لگا رہتا ہے، وہ یہ بھی الزام لگاتے ہیں کہ سرکاران معاملات میں منھ بھرائی اور خاموشی کے رویہ پر عمل کرتی ہے۔

اس طرح کا زہریلا پروپیگنڈہ قومی یکجہتی اور بھائی چارہ کے لئے زہر قاتل ہے۔ ہم سب کو چاہیے کہ اسکو کامیاب نہ ہونے دیں۔

باب سوم

ہندوستان - متعدد تہذیبوں کا گہوارہ

ڈاکٹر ریتا باگچی

ہمارے ملک ہندوستان میں زندگی کے ہر شعبہ میں رنگارنگی پائی جاتی ہے، یہاں کئی تہذیبیں اور کلچر پائے جاتے ہیں، بہت سی زبانیں اور بولیاں بولی جاتی ہیں۔ مختلف مذہبوں کے ماننے والے رہتے ہیں۔ نہ معلوم کتنی ذاتیں، قبیلے اور نسلی گروہ اپنے مخصوص رسم و رواج، رہن سہن، ادب اور موسیقی کی بنا پر اپنی شناخت رکھتے ہیں۔ اس عظیم ملک میں اختلاف کی یہ کثرت ملک کی وحدت کے ساتھ ایک انمول تحفہ ہے جس نے اسکا نام دنیا میں اونچا کر رکھا ہے۔ سماج میں گوناگوں تہذیبوں یا کلچر کی بہار بڑی دلکش اور قابلِ قدر ہے۔ ہندوستان کی پرانی تاریخ اور تہذیبوں کی نشوونما کی کہانی بڑی دلچسپ اور سبق آموز ہے جو ہم کو یاد دلاتی ہے کہ باوجود اتنے زیادہ اختلافات کے یہ ملک ہمیشہ ایک رہا اور آج ہماری فیڈرل یونین میں مختلف قسم کی اکائیاں (ریاستیں) اپنی اپنی پہچان کے ساتھ مختلف تہذیبوں کو ملکی اتحاد اور ایکتا کے پس منظر میں پیش کر رہی ہیں۔ بلا شبہ کبھی کبھی ان اختلافات کی وجہ سے تصادم یا کشمکش کی صورت پیدا ہو جاتی ہے مگر بقول ہمارے عظیم ہر دل عزیز لیڈر پنڈت جواہر لال نہرو "ہمارا ملکی اور قومی اتحاد کہیں

باہر سے نہیں آیا بلکہ اسکی بنیاد رواداری اور اشتراک کے قدیم رواج، جو یہاں کے لوگوں نے اپنی خوشی اور مرضی سے قبول کیا ہے، پر ہے۔''

یہ واقعہ ہے کہ ہندوستانی فیڈ ریشن، متعدد تہذیبوں اور شناختوں کا ایک متحدہ پلیٹ فارم ہے جہاں کوہ ہمالیہ سے لے کر کنیا کماری اور پنجاب سے لے کر شمال مشرقی علاقوں تک مذہب، زبان، رسم و رواج، رہن سہن کے نمونے سماج کے معاشی، سماجی اور تہذیبی دائروں میں جیتے جاگتے اور جگمگاتے نظر آتے ہیں۔ متحدہ قومیت کے اس دھارے نے سیکولر طرز حکومت، سماجی انصاف، رواداری اور انسان دوستی کو جنم دیا اور پروان چڑھایا یہ کوئی معمولی کارنامہ نہیں ہے۔

ہمیں فخر ہے کہ ہمارے ملک میں ایک سے زیادہ کلچر، مذہب اور زبانیں موجود ہیں جن کا قومی سطح پر اعتراف اور احترام کیا جاتا ہے۔ اسکی وجہ سے انسانیت اور اخلاقی قدروں کو بڑا فائدہ پہنچا۔ تعصب، تفریق اور نفرت کے جذبات اور محرکات کو روکنے میں ہمارے ملک کے تہذیبی اور سماجی اختلافات نے بڑی مدد کی اور ایک دوسرے کی شناخت اور سمجھنے میں بڑی آسانی ہوئی۔

آج ہم کو افراد اور مختلف معاشی وسماجی اور تہذیبی گروہوں کی شناخت، ان کو تسلیم کرنے اور ان کے ساتھ کام کرنے میں کوئی دقّت نہیں ہوتی اور باہمی ربط اور دوستی کا سلسلہ ملک کے طول وعرض میں جاری اور ساری ہے۔ اس سے بڑھ کر خوشی اور اطمینان کی کیا بات ہوسکتی ہے کہ ہندوستان کے عوام کی مختلف خصوصیات نے ہماری قومی شناخت کو نہایت مستحکم اور دل پذیر بنا دیا ہے۔

ہمارا قومی تہذیبی ورثہ ہزاروں سال کا پرانا ہے۔ دنیا کے مختلف لوگوں کی تہذیب، مذہب، زبان اور رسم و رواج نے ہمارے ملک کے تہذیبی و سماجی ارتقا پر بڑا اثر ڈالا ہے۔ جو اچھا بھی ہے اور برا بھی، یہاں کے پرانے رہنے والے دراوڑوں نے ہندو تہذیب وتمدن کی بنیاد ڈالی جسکو آریوں نے مختلف نظریوں اور صحت مند روایات سے سنوارا اور سجایا۔ ویدک ادب، وادیٔ سندھ کی تہذیب اور اسکے بعد ساکا، ہُن، کش، بدھ، جین مت، یونانیوں، مسلمانوں اور عیسائیوں سے میل جول اور ان کے اثرات سے ہندوستان کا ملا جلا کلچر پیدا ہوا جو آج تک پورے طور پر تابندہ اور پائندہ ہے۔ تاریخ ہمیں یہ بھی بتاتی ہے کہ شروع میں ہندو ویدک دھرم بڑا سیدھا سادھا تھا رفتہ رفتہ اس میں نئی چیزیں جوڑی گئیں، کچھ خرابیاں بھی پیدا ہوئیں جنکے خلاف لوگوں نے احتجاج کیا۔ بدھ، جین اور سکھ مذہب پیدا ہوئے، نئے نئے فرقے اور تنظیموں کا جنم ہوا مگر ملک کی مرکزیت قائم رہی، ذات پات، ہندو فلسفہ، بھگتی تحریک اور ہندو مت پر دوسرے سامی مذہبوں کے اثرات نے بھی ہندوستان کے مخلوط کلچر کو بہت کچھ دیا۔

ہندوستان میں مذہبوں کے تعدد (کثرت) نے بھی اہم اثرات ڈالے ہیں۔ انہوں نے ہندوستان کے سماجی اور ثقافتی زندگی کے بنیادی اصولوں کے بنانے میں مدد کی ہے۔ اس سلسلہ میں دنیا کے آٹھ بڑے مذہبوں، ہندو دھرم، اسلام، عیسائیت، سکھ ازم، بدھ مت، جین مت، یہودیت اور زرتشتی (پارسیوں) کے نام ہمارے سامنے آتے ہیں۔ جن کے عقیدے، بنیادی اصول، عبادت کا طریقہ، سچائی اخلاقی آداب اور اطوار معاشرت ایک دوسرے سے مختلف ہونے کے باوجود آپس میں کچھ مشترک باتیں

بھی رکھتے ہیں اور ایک دوسرے کی شناخت، احترام اور رواداری کے ساتھ کرتے ہیں۔ اس سلسلہ میں ہندوؤں کی بھگتی تحریک، اسلام میں صوفیوں کی روایات اور گرونانک کے اصولوں نے اجتماعی زندگی اور سماجی رواداری اور خوشگوار تعلقات پیدا کرنے میں خاصا حصہ لیا ہے۔ ہندوستان میں مذہب کے زیر اثر تقریباً زندگی کا ہر دائرہ ہوتا ہے اور ہر مذہب کے ماننے والے برابری اور عقیدہ کی آزادی کے حقوق کے مالک ہوتے ہیں۔ ان کا اپنا عبادت کا طریقہ، رہنے سہنے کے طریقے، رواج، عائلی قانون اور اپنی تنظیمیں ہوتی ہیں جن کے ذریعہ وہ اپنے مذہب اور سماجی وتہذیبی اقدار کی حفاظت اور فروغ کا کام انجام دیتے ہیں۔ ہندوستان کے آئین نے سیکولر بنیاد پر ان کے پورے تحفظ کی ضمانت دی ہے اور سب مذہبوں کو برابری کا درجہ عطا کیا ہے۔

ہندوستان میں اسلام کی آمد سے تہذیب وتمدن اور سماجی زندگی بڑا گہرا اثر پڑا۔ کیونکہ اسلام کے ایک آفاقی مذہب ہونے کی وجہ سے مختلف نسلوں، رنگوں اور متضاد خصوصیات رکھنے والے لوگوں نے اسے قبول کیا۔ مثلاً عرب ایرانی، افغانی، افریقی، یوروپین، ایشیائی وغیرہ۔ یہ سمجھنا صحیح نہیں کہ مسلمانوں کے آنے سے قبل ہندوستان میں صرف ہندو ہی رہتے تھے۔ ہندوستان کی قدیم ترین تاریخ بتاتی ہے کہ شہنشاہ اشوک بدھ مت کا پیروتھا اور ملک کے مختلف حصوں میں بدھ خانقاہیں اور مٹھ موجود تھے۔ اسلام سے قبل عیسائی پارسی اور یہودی ہندوستان آچکے تھے مگر یہ بات بھی بے شک درست ہے کہ اسلام کے مقابلہ میں کسی مذہب نے اتنے گہرے اثرات نہیں چھوڑے اور مسلمان

صدیوں سے اپنے ہندو ہم وطنوں کے ساتھ صلح و آشتی سے رہ رہے ہیں۔ مغلوں نے اپنے وطن کو بھلا کر ہندوستان میں اپنی سلطنت قائم کی اور یہاں کی زندگی میں خوب گھل مل گئے۔ ہندوستان کے کلچر میں جو ان کا عظیم حصہ ہے اسے کبھی بھلایا نہیں جا سکتا۔ ہندوستان میں مسلم حکومتوں اور اسلام نے بڑے دور رس اثرات چھوڑے، آبادی کے بڑے حصہ نے اونچ نیچ اور سماجی برائیوں سے تنگ آکر اسلام قبول کیا۔ مساوات، عدل اور حقوق العباد کی پابندی نے اسلام کو خوب پھیلایا۔ اور مسلمان سرداروں، تاجروں ہنرمندوں اور فوجیوں نے یہاں کے پچھڑے اور کمزور طبقے کے لوگوں کی ہر طرح سے سماجی، معاشی، روحانی اور علمی ترقی حاصل کرنے میں مدد کی۔ مغلیہ سلطنت میں ادب، تعمیر، موسیقی اور دیگر فنون لطیفہ کی ترقی کے ساتھ معاشی خوشحالی، مساوات اور رواداری کی فراوانی نے بڑے اچھے اثرات مرتب کئے۔ سوامی وویکانند نے ہندوستان کے اسلامی عہد کو تہذیب و ترقی کا زرّیں دور قرار دیا ہے۔ اسی طرح مشہور مؤرخ تاراچند اور مجمدار نے رسم و رواج، کھانے پینے، لباس، رہنے سہنے، ادب اور مختلف علوم وفنون میں مسلمانوں کے کلیدی کردار کا ذکر تعریف و تحسین کے ساتھ کیا ہے۔ خود مسلمانوں نے مقامی اثرات اپنے رہن سہن اور زندگی کے دوسرے شعبوں میں قبول کئے جسکی وجہ سے مخلوط یا گنگا جمنی ہندوستانی کلچر وجود میں آیا۔ تاج محل اور دوسری تاریخی عمارتوں میں اسلامی اثرات کے ساتھ ہندو، بدھ، جین اور ایرانی خصوصیات کی بھی جھلک نظر آتی ہے۔ اس ملے جلے ہندوستان کے کلچر میں مختلف علاقوں کے رسم و رواج، زبان، مذہب وغیرہ کی نمائندگی بھی ملتی ہے جو ہر طرح قابل تعریف ہے۔ ظاہر ہے کلچر یا

تمدن زبردستی کسی پر مسلط نہیں کیا جاسکتا، یہی وجہ ہے کہ اتنا عرصہ گزر جانے کے بعد بھی ملک کے چپہ چپہ میں اختلاف میں اشتراک اور قومی ایکتا کے نمونے ملتے ہیں۔ عام طور پر علاقائی عصبیت کو علیحدگی پسندی اور لامرکزیت کے ساتھ وابستہ کیا جاتا ہے۔ مگر ہندوستان کی تاریخ اور روایات نے اس تاثر کو غلط ثابت کیا۔ یہاں مختلف علاقوں اور ریاستوں نے اپنی تعلیمی اور معاشی پچھڑے پن کے خلاف بے شک احتجاج کیا اور تحریکیں چلائیں اور ہمارے دستور اور انتظامیہ نے ان کی طرف توجہ کی اور ان کی شکایتوں کو دور کرنے کی ہمدردانہ کوشیش بھی کیں۔ رواداری اور انصاف کا تقاضا بھی یہی ہے کہ قومی مفادات کے تحت ملک کے سب ہی علاقوں کو تعلیمی معاشی اور سماجی ترقی کے جائز مواقع برابری کے ساتھ فراہم کئے جائیں۔

زبانون اور بولیوں کا مسئلہ:۔ زبان ایک ایسا عام فہم ذریعہ ہے جس سے ہم علم و دانش، تاریخ، تہذیب، سماجیات اور معاشیات بلکہ زندگی کے ہر شعبہ کے متعلق معلومات حاصل کر سکتے اور دوسروں تک پہنچا سکتے ہیں۔ ہمارے ملک میں 325 زبانین اور 25 رسم الخط موجود ہیں جن میں سے اٹھارہ زبانوں کو دستور نے قومی زبانوں کا درجہ دیا ہے اور باقی کو علاقائی زبانیں قرار دیا ہے، جن کے ذریعہ تعلیم آسانی سے مادری زبان میں دی جاسکتی ہے۔ ہمارے ملک کی سرکاری زبان ہندی کے ساتھ انگریزی بھی ہے مگر ہندی کے کٹّر حامی حبّ الوطنی کے نام پر چاہتے ہیں کہ صرف ہندی دیوناگری رسم الخط کے ساتھ سرکاری زبان قرار دی جائے۔ ظاہر ہے کہ یہ بات غیر ہندی داں ریاستوں اور لوگوں کو پسند نہیں اور انصاف و معقولیت سے میل نہیں کھاتی۔

عقل اور انصاف کی بات یہ ہے کہ ہندی، انگریزی اور علاقائی زبانون کے تعاون سے کام چلانا چاہیے اور اسی طریقے سے ملک میں نظم نسق تعلیم اور ایک دوسرے کو سمجھنے کا مناسب اور موثر انتظام کیا جا سکتا ہے۔

ذات پات اور قبیلوں کا مسئلہ:۔ ہمارے ملک کے سماجی ڈھانچہ میں ذات پات اور گوتر خاص اہمیت رکھتے ہیں۔ جن کا براہ راست تعلق شادی بیاہ، پیشہ، تقسیم کار اور رہن سہن سے ہے۔ اسکی بنیادی خرابیاں چھوت چھات پیدائش کی بنا پر ناجائز استحصال اور اونچی ذات والوں کا نچلی ذاتوں سے غیر انسانی اور ظالمانہ سلوک ہیں جو برسوں سے چلی آ رہی ہیں۔ اس صورت حال کو بدلنے کی سخت اور فوری ضرورت ہے۔ اونچی ذات والوں کو اپنی غلط روش بدلنا چاہے اور ملک چلانے والوں کا فرض ہے کہ وہ نچلی ذات والوں یا دلتوں کی خراب تعلیمی و معاشی حالت کو درست کریں اور ان کو برابر کے جائز حقوق دیں۔

اسی کے ساتھ قبائلی لوگوں کا بھی مسئلہ اہم ہے جو عام قومی دھارے سے الگ ہیں۔ اپنے مخصوص رسم و رواج اور علیحدگی پسند احساسات رکھتے ہیں۔ وہ پسماندگی، جہالت اور کچھ سماجی خرابیوں کا شکار ہیں۔ ہمارا فرض ہے کہ ان کی اصلاح کے لئے ضروری قدم اٹھائیں۔ ان کے قبائلی ورثہ اور روایات کی حفاظت کے ساتھ ان کو پورا موقعہ دیا جائے کہ وہ ہر قسم کی ترقی کر کے قومی دھارے میں اپنی جگہ بنائیں۔ انگریزوں کے چلے جانے کے بعد ہندوستان آزاد جمہوریہ بن گیا ہے۔ اسکی ذمہ داری ہے کہ ملک کی اقلیتوں اور پچھڑے طبقوں کی فلاح و بہبود کے لئے خصوصی پروگرام مرتب کرے۔

ہمارے دستور میں اسکی پوری گنجائش رکھی گئی ہے کہ ملک کے مختلف طبقوں کی زبان، مذہب، رسم ورواج اور تہذیبی خصوصیات کی حفاظت کی جائے اور ان کو قومی ورثہ اور مخلوط کلچر میں عزت ووقار کی جگہ دی جائے۔

آج ہر طرف انسانی حقوق اور اقدار کی حفاظت کا مطالبہ ہو رہا ہے۔ ہندوستان میں بھی یہ مسئلہ بڑی اہمیت رکھتا ہے۔ ملک کا فیڈرل اور مرکزی کردار اس بات کا تقاضہ کرتا ہے کہ سیاسی اعتبار سے تو ملک ایک اور متحد رہے لیکن تمدن وتہذیب کے دائرہ میں اختلاف کی عام اجازت ہو۔ ریاست کا فرض ہے کہ وہ اختلاف میں اشتراک کے زرین اور ہمہ گیر اصول پر مستعدی سے عمل کرے۔

افسوس کی بات ہے کہ ہمارے ملک میں اس سلسلہ میں قول اور فعل میں خاصا فرق پایا جاتا ہے۔ موقعہ پرستی، بددیانتی، خودغرضی، ذات پات کے کٹرپن اور دوسرے مجرمانہ محرکات کی وجہ سے قومی یکجہتی اور ہمارے رنگا رنگ مخلوط کلچر کو خطرہ لاحق ہو رہا ہے۔ مذہب اور زبان کے تعصب اور انتہا پسندی نے مذاہب اور زبانوں کی کثرت کے فوائد کو دھندلا کر دیا ہے۔ اس فتنہ کو کچلنے کے کی سخت ضرورت ہے۔ حالات نازک اور خراب ضرور ہیں مگر ناامیدی کی بات نہیں۔ تاریکی کے ماحول میں امید کی کرن موجود ہے یعنی مناسب اصلاحی قدم اٹھا کر اس طرح کی الجھنوں کو دور کیا جا سکتا ہے جسکی ذمہ داری اس ملک کے سب ہی شہریوں کی ہے۔

باب چہارم:

مساوات پسند سوسائٹی میں برابری کا مفہوم

پروفیسرعبدالرحیم پی وجاپور

صدیوں سے پیغمبروں، مذہبی قائدوں، فلسفیوں، مدبّرین، دانشوروں اور سیاسی مفکّروں میں بحث چلی آرہی ہے کہ مساوات پسند سوسائٹی ہے کیا چیز اور اسے کیوں کر قائم کیا جاسکتا ہے؟ اسکے بنیادی اصول کیا ہیں؟ مساوات کی عملی شکل کیا ہے اور اسکے نافذ کرنے کے لئے کیا صرف مثبت کاروائی کرنا ضروری ہے یا تفریق اور دباؤ سے بھی کام لینا ضروری ہے؟ آج بھی انسانی حقوق کے پرجوش وکیل ان سوالات میں الجھے ہوئے ہیں۔ سب سے پہلے ہمکو سمجھ لینا چاہیے کہ مساوات پسند سوسائٹی اور مساوات یا برابری کے اصل معنی یا مفہوم ہیں کیا؟ یہ لفظ انگریزی زبان میں فرنچ زبان سے آئے، جن کا مطلب یہ ہے کہ سب ہی باشندوں کو کسی ملک میں پیدا ہونے کے بعد ایک جیسے سیاسی، معاشی سماجی اور شہری حقوق حاصل ہوں اور وہ مملکت، مذہب اور قانون کی نظر میں بالکل برابر سمجھے جاتے ہوں۔

آج کی سیاسی فضا میں انسانوں کی برابری کا مسئلہ بڑی اہمیت رکھتا ہے۔ نابرابری اور اونچ نیچ ملک میں انتشار، بدامنی یہاں تک انقلاب لاسکتی ہے۔ مگر برابری

کے نظریہ کی عملی شکل کے بارے میں اختلافات بلکہ متضاد خیالات پائے جاتے ہیں۔ لوگوں میں برابری ذرائع، صلاحیت، فلاح و بہبود، عزت، احترام اور یکساں موقعوں کی فراہمی کے ذریعہ لائی جاسکتی ہے۔ اور اس سلسلہ میں ٹکراؤ یا کسی ایک کو ترجیح دینے کا فیصلہ کرنا پڑتا ہے۔ نامور فرانسیسی مفکّر روسو کا کہنا ہے کہ انسانوں میں نابرابری دو طرح کی پائی جاتی ہے، ایک تو قدرتی طریقہ کی، جس کا تعلق عمر، صحت، جسمانی و ذہنی طاقتوں سے ہوتا ہے اور دوسری رواجی اور اختیاری، جو دولت، طاقت اور عزت و احترام کے اعتبار سے پائی جاتی ہے۔

پہلی قسم کی نابرابری قدرت کی طرف سے ہوتی ہے اور دوسری انسانوں کی بنائی ہوئی۔ اس قسم کی نابرابری اور اس وقت کے سماج، حکومت اور انصاف کے غلط رویّہ کا نتیجہ ۱۷۸۹ میں فرانس میں دیکھا گیا جس کے بعد وہاں شہریوں کے حقوق کا چارٹر تیار کیا گیا۔ اس سلسلہ میں روسو کی زبان سے یہ انقلاب آفرین فقرہ یا نعرہ نکلا ''سب انسان برابری اور آزادی کے حقوق لے کر آزاد پیدا ہوتے ہیں۔ مگر سماج ان کو تفریق اور اونچ نیچ کی زنجیروں میں جکڑ لیتا ہے۔''

اس بارے میں کچھ اور مشہور سیاسی فاضلوں کے خیالات پیش ہیں۔

آرینسن کا کہنا ہے کہ ''سیاسی مساوات جمہوری شہری حقوق سے بڑھ کر وسیع اور طاقتور ہوتی ہے جس میں ہر شخص کو بالکل یکساں سماجی اور معاشی حقوق حاصل ہوتے ہین۔ جس کی بنیاد فلاح و بہبود کے وسائل، اور صلاحیتوں کو اپنی مرضی کے مطابق بر سرکار لانے پر ہوتی ہے''۔ ایک دوسرے مفکّر جان راول نے انصاف پر مبنی معتدل مساوات

پسندی کا نظریہ پیش کیا ہے۔اس نے تین اصولوں کا سہارا لیا ہے۔

(۱)۔ سیاست میں حصہ لینے، رائے عقیدہ اور قانون کے سامنے برابری کے آزادانہ حقوق۔

(۲)۔ لیاقت بڑھانے، عہدے اور ذمہ داری حاصل کرنے کے موقعوں کی یکساں فراہمی۔

(۳)۔ سماج کے پچھڑے طبقوں کو فائدہ پہنچانے کے لئے کچھ امتیازات یا تفریق کی اجازت ان کا کہنا ہے کہ یہ تینوں اصول سماج کی بہتری کے لئے ایک زنجیر کی کڑیوں کی طرح ہیں اور یہ ضروری ہے کہ کمزور کڑی کو درست کر کے ہمیشہ زنجیر کو صحیح اور مضبوط حالت میں رکھا جائے۔

راٹلڈ ڈارکن کا کہنا ہے کہ ''مساوات کا دارو مدار فلاح و بہود اوران کے وسائل دونوں کی اچھی تقسیم پر ہوتا ہے اوراسکی دوشکلیں ہیں پہلی صورت میں لوگوں میں وسائل کی تقسیم اس طرح کی جاتی ہے کہ فلاح و بہتری کے اعتبار سے ہرایک کو برابر کا حصہ ملے، اس سلسلہ میں لوگوں کی پسند اور حوصلوں کی کارفرمائی ہوتی ہے اوران کا لحاظ رکھا جاتا ہے۔ دوسری شکل میں لوگوں میں برابر، برابر وسائل کی تقسیم یہ مان کر کی جاتی ہے کہ وہ سب ہر لحاظ سے برابر اور یکساں ہیں''۔ وہ خود دوسری شکل کی تائید کرتے ہیں۔

ہندوستان کے نوبل انعام یافتہ عالم امرتیا سین نے مساوات کے تمام نظریوں کا غور سے مطالعہ کرنے کے بعد یہ بتایا کہ ہرنظریہ میں کچھ نہ کچھ کمی یا نقص پایا جاتا ہے۔

اس لئے ان سب کو ملا کر انہوں نے ایک نظریہ برابری کی بنیاد پر اہلیت کا قائم کیا جس کے مطابق لوگ مختلف چیزوں کے استعمال سے برابری کا حصہ پا سکتے ہیں۔

آج سماج میں برابری لانے کے لئے سوشلزم، کمیونزم، انسانی حقوق اور فلاحی ریاست کے تخیل اور تحریکیں دنیا میں موجود ہیں جن میں لوگوں کو قانونی، سماجی، معاشی اور سیاسی برابری کے حقوق دیئے جانے کا دعوی کیا جاتا ہے۔ سوشلزم اور کمیونزم میں نجی ملکیت کی جگہ ریاست کو وسائل پیدائش کا مالک تسلیم کیا گیا اور افراد کو کام کرنے، سماجی تحفظ تعلیم حاصل کرنے، حفظان صحت اور مکان رکھنے کے حقوق کی ضمانت دی جاتی ہے۔ چنانچہ سوویت روس میں 1917 اور 1991 کے درمیان اس پالیسی پر عمل کیا گیا جو بڑی حد تک کامیاب ثابت ہوا۔ لیکن مشرقی یورپ کے دوسرے کمیونسٹ ملکوں میں ایسا نہیں ہوا کیونکہ وہاں ریاست نے شہریوں کو سیاسی اور مذہبی حقوق کی پوری آزادی نہیں دی۔ کچھ سرمایہ دار مملکتوں نے سماجی تحفظ اور مذہب کی آزادی کے مساوی حقوق اپنے شہریوں کو اس لئے دیئے تاکہ وہ کمیونسٹ طرز کا انقلاب لانے کی کوششوں سے باز رہیں۔

دنیا کے بڑے مذہبوں میں مساوات کی تعلیم:۔

دنیا کے بڑے مذہبوں، عیسائیت، اسلام اور ہندومت میں انسانوں کی برابری کو تسلیم کیا گیا ہے۔ ہندومت کے اپنشدوں اور بھگوت گیتا میں اس بنیادی عقیدہ کا اظہار کیا گیا ہے کہ خدا ہر جگہ اور ہر شئے میں موجود ہے اور اسکے بنائے ہوئے انسانوں

میں کوئی فرق نہیں پایا جاتا۔ ذات پات کا زور پکڑنے سے پہلے ہندو تعلیمات میں سب مذہبوں کے ایک ہونے اور انسانیت کی ایک برادری ہونے کا ذکر کثرت سے ملتا ہے۔ عیسائیت کے نقطہ نظر سے بائبل میں تمام عورتوں اور مردوں کو، خواہ وہ کسی نسل، معاشی یا سماجی گروہ سے تعلق رکھتے ہوں، حضرت عیسٰی کے پیرو ہونے اور ایک دوسرے کے برابر ہونے پر زور دیا گیا ہے اور یہ کہا گیا ہے کہ خدا سب انسانوں سے یکساں طور پر محبت کرتا ہے اور ان میں جنس، نسل، مرتبہ کے لحاظ سے کوئی فرق نہیں کرتا۔ لیکن افسوس ہے ہندومت اور عیسائیت دونوں میں ان تعلیمات پر عمل نہیں کیا جاتا اور دلت خواتین کے ساتھ اچھا سلوک نہیں کیا جاتا۔ اسلام نے مساوات اور عالمی برادری کے تصور کو عام کر کے پیش کیا اور وہ رنگ یا نسل یا جنس کی بنا پر انسانوں میں کوئی تفریق یا امتیاز نہیں برتتا۔ اسلام نے ہر انسان کو خواہ وہ مسلم ہو یا غیر مسلم اپنے قانون کے تحت برابری کا درجہ دیا ہے اور غیر مسلموں کے حقوق کا پورا تحفظ کیا ہے۔ میدان عرفات کے آخری خطبہ میں اللہ کے آخری رسول حضرت محمد مصطفٰے صلے اللہ علیہ وسلم نے یہ اعلان کیا، ''اے لوگو تمہارا معبود خدائے واحد ہے جس نے تمکو حضرت آدم کی اولاد میں خاک سے پیدا کیا، تم میں سے کسی کو اسکے رنگ، نسل یا دولت و مرتبہ کی بنا پر فضیلت نہیں، کیونکہ اسکا تعلق صرف اچھے اعمال سے ہے''۔ اسلامی ریاست اور سماج نے پوری دنیا میں انسانوں کی مساوات کے اصول پر عمل کیا جس کا اعتراف آرنلڈ ٹائن بی اور دوسرے مؤرخوں اور سماجی و سیاسی مفکرین نے کیا ہے۔ شادی بیاہ، عہدوں کی تقسیم اور عورتوں کے حقوق کے سلسلہ میں اسلام نے مساوات کے اصول پر بڑے اچھے طریقہ سے عمل کیا ہے۔

مساوات انسانی حقوق اور اقلیتوں کے حقوق:۔

آج کی مساوات پسند سوسائٹی میں انسانی اور اقلیتوں کے حقوق کو بنیادی اہمیت حاصل ہے۔ جسکا اظہار اقوام متحدہ کی جنرل اسمبلی نے 10 دسمبر 1948 کے اپنے اعلان میں اس طرح کیا۔''سب انسان آزاد پیدا ہوتے ہیں اور انہیں انسانی حقوق اور عزت برابری کے درجہ پر حاصل ہوتے ہیں۔ ان کو چاہیے کہ وہ اپنی عقل اور ضمیر کے مطابق ایک دوسرے سے بھائی چارہ کا برتاؤ کریں۔'' انسانی حقوق کی مساوات کا مطلب یہ ہے کہ تمام انسان قانون کی نظر میں برابر ہیں اور ان کو غلامی، ناجائز گرفتاری، استحصال سے آزادی، ووٹ دینے کا حق، اپنے عقیدہ، کلچر، زبان، کام کرنے، آنے جانے، بولنے لکھنے پڑھنے، صحت تعلیم اچھی معیار زندگی کے حقوق یکساں درجہ کے حاصل ہوں گے۔ اس اعلان کی توثیق 1966 میں دو بین الاقوامی معاہدوں شہری اور سیاسی حقوق پر بین الاقوامی میثاق (ICCPR) اور معاشی، سماجی اور ثقافتی حقوق پر بین الاقوامی میثاق (ICESCR) کے ذریعہ کی گئی۔ اور جملہ انسانی حقوق ہر شخص کو بلاتفریقِ مذہب، رنگ، نسل، جنس و زبان عطا کئے گئے اور اسکے لئے کسی قسم کی سیاسی، قومی یا سماجی یا جائداد، پیدائش و مرتبہ کی کوئی شرط نہیں رکھی گئی۔ اقلیتوں کے لئے خاص طور پر یہ ضمانت دی گئی کہ ان کو عقیدہ، زبان، رائے کی آزادی کے ساتھ جان و مال کے تحفظ اپنی تہذیبی و سماجی شناخت قائم رکھنے، تعلیمی ادارے کھولنے اور انصاف حاصل کرنے کے حقوق حاصل ہونگے جو مساوات پسند سوسائٹی کا لازمی حصہ ہوتے ہیں۔ اس ضمن میں مہاتما گاندھی کا قول بڑی اہمیت رکھتا ہے۔''کسی تہذیب کی اچھائی برائی کا فیصلہ اس کے اپنی اقلیتوں کے برتاؤ سے کیا جا سکتا ہے۔''

مثبت امتیازی رویہ اور مساوات :۔

غیر انسانی حرکتوں یا نسلی وسماجی تعصب اور زیادتیوں کو روکنے اور ان سے پیدا ہونے والی خرابیوں کو ختم کرنے کے لئے بعض صورتوں میں بطور علاج امتیاز یا تفریق کے رویہ کو اپنا پڑتا ہے مگر چونکہ اسکا استعمال بطور علاج اور نابرابری کو روکنے کے لئے ہوتا ہے۔اس لئے اسکو درست اور معقول قرار دیا جاتا ہے اور اسکو مثبت قدم کہا جاتا ہے۔

اقوام متحدہ کی انسانی حقوق کی کونسل کی مشادرتی کمیٹی نے نسل، جنس یا مذہب کی بنا پر کی جانے والی غلط کاروائیوں کے خلاف اس طریقہ پر عمل کرنے کی ہدایت کی ہے تاکہ متاثرہ افراد یا گروہوں کی اشک شوئی کی جائے اور ان کو بنیادی انسانی حقوق بلا روک ٹوک کے ملتے رہیں۔لیکن ان اقدامات کو عارضی طور پر جب تک ضرورت ہو استعمال کرنا چاہیے۔کیونکہ یہ سخت کاروائی صرف خاص صورت حال میں کی جاتی ہے اور ظاہری طور پر مساوات اور انسانیت دوستی سے میل نہیں کھاتی۔ بین الاقوامی قانون کے ماہرین اور سیاسی عالموں نے کہا ہے کہ یہ کاروائی اقلیتی گروہوں کے نقصانات کی تلافی اور ان کے انسانی حقوق کی بازیابی کے لئے عارضی طور یعنی مختصر مدت کے لئے کرنی چاہیے مثلاً زبان، مذہبی اور تعلیمی اداردں کے تحفظ و قیام یا نشستوں کے محفوظ کرنے کے لئے اور یہ کاروائی معقول اور محدود پیانہ پر ہونا چاہیے۔ یہ وضاحت اقوام متحدہ کے اعلان کی دفعات 4 اور 8 میں کی گئی ہے۔مثلاً عورتوں کے خلاف تفریق وامتیاز کا سلوک ختم کرنے کے لئے اور اقلیتوں کو مواقع فراہم کرنے کے لئے ایسی کاروائی اسی وقت تک کی جانا چاہیے جب تک یہ مقصد پورا نہ ہوجائے۔ ہمارے ملک ہندوستان نے ICESCR کے بین الاقوامی معاہدہ کی دفعہ 2 میں یہ وضاحتی پیراگراف بڑھانے کی

تجویز پیش کی کہ کسی بھی سماجی یا معاشی طور پر پچھڑے ہوئے طبقہ کو آگے بڑھنے اور دوسروں کے دوش بدوش ترقی کرنے کے اقدامات کو مساوات یا انصاف کے خلاف نہ سمجھا جائے۔'' چنانچہ اس تجویز کو حقوق انسانی کمیٹی نے دوسرے بین الاقوامی معاہدہ کی دفعہ 26 کے تحت یہ اعلان شامل کرلیا ہے کہ کبھی کبھی مساوات کے اصول کے خلاف کسی پچھڑے ہوئے طبقہ یا گروہ کو ان کے جائز حقوق دلوانے کے لئے ریاست کو مثبت انداز کے قدم ایک خاص مدت اور مصلحت کے لئے اٹھانا پڑتے ہیں، ان کو مساوات یا انصاف کے خلاف تصور نہ کیا جائے۔ یہ اقدام قانونی، عدالتی یا انتظامی قسم کے ہوسکتے ہیں جو کسی اقلیت کے مذہب، زبان اور کلچر کی حفاظت کے لئے اٹھائے جاتے ہیں اور ان کو غیر منصفانہ یا نامناسب قرار نہیں دیا جانا چاہیے۔

بین الاقوامی عدالت عالیہ نے بھی اپنے بعض فیصلوں میں خصوصاً جنوب مغربی افریقہ کے مقدموں میں اس اصول کی تائید کی ہے کہ قانون کی نظر میں برابری کا تقاضا ہے کہ جو لوگ کمزور اور پیچھے رہ گئے ہیں ان کے ساتھ امتیازی سلوک برتا جائے۔

عورت و مرد کی مساوات کا مسئلہ:۔

مساوات پسند سوسائٹی کی بنیاد مرد وزن کی برابری پر رکھی گئی ہے۔ اس میں عورتوں کو سماجی، سیاسی اور قانونی دائروں میں مردوں کے مساوی حقوق عطا کئے گئے ہیں اور انہیں گھریلو تشدد، صغرسنی کی شادی، جنسی تفریق اور چھیڑ چھاڑ، نازیبا برتاؤ، نکاح اور طلاق میں زیادتیوں کے خلاف تحفظ دیا گیا ہے اور مردوں کے برابر حقوق دئے گئے ہیں۔ عورتوں کی نمائندگی ملک کے مختلف دائروں میں نظر آرہی ہے چنانچہ اس وقت

ہندوستان کی صدر، اسپیکر، مقننہ عدلیہ، انتظامیہ اور پرائیویٹ سیکٹر میں اعلیٰ عہدوں پر خواتین فائز ہیں اور ان کی تعلیم کی طرف خاص توجہ دی جارہی ہے۔ دنیا کے مختلف ملکوں میں عورتوں کے ساتھ زمانہ قدیم سے غیر منصفانہ اور نابرابری کا سلوک کیا جاتا تھا، ان کو ووٹ دینے کا حق، وراثت میں حصہ، عہدوں اور ملازمت میں جگہ نہیں دی جاتی تھی اور ان کا ذکر تحقیر آمیز لہجہ میں کتابوں، اخباروں، کہاوتوں یہاں تک مذہبی تقریروں میں کیا جاتا تھا اور اسکے خلاف دنیا کے طول و عرض میں احتجاج کیا گیا اور خواتین کو مساوی حقوق دینے کی تحریکیں چلائی گئیں۔ رومن عہد میں عورتوں کی خرید فروخت عام تھی، مسیحی کلیسا میں عورتوں کو ذلیل اور ابدی گنہگار سمجھا جاتا تھا، قدیم ہندوستان اور اسلام سے پہلے عرب میں بچیوں کو زندہ دفن کردیا جاتا تھا۔ چین، جاپان، اٹلی، اسپین میں عورتوں کو مارنے پیٹنے کا عام رواج تھا اور ان کے خلاف طرح طرح کی دل شکن کہاوتیں اور محاورے استعمال کئے جاتے تھے۔ منو کے ضابطہ قانون، بھگوت گیتا اور مہابھارت میں عورتوں کا شمار دلتوں، معذور اور نااہل طبقوں میں کیا جاتا تھا، بیوہ اور بے اولاد عورتوں کی زندگی بڑی تلخ ہوتی تھی۔ لیکن اب حالات بالکل بدل چکے ہیں اور عورتوں کے ساتھ عزت اور انصاف کا برتاؤ کیا جاتا ہے۔

قانونی اور سیاسی مساوات :۔

قانونی مساوات یعنی قانون کی نظر میں سب انسانوں کے برابر ہونے کا نظریہ خاصی جدوجہد اور دشواریوں کے بعد دنیا میں مقبول ہوا۔ زمانہ قدیم میں اسکا تصور بھی نہیں کیا جاسکتا تھا۔ پراچین بھارت میں منوسمرتی اور ہندو قانون ذات پات کی بنیاد پر

کھل کر انسانوں میں تفریق کرتا تھا اور ہر معاملہ میں اعلیٰ ذات (برہمنوں، چھتریوں وغیرہ) کے لوگوں کو ترجیح دی جاتی تھی۔ شودروں کے ساتھ بڑی ناانصافی اور بے رحمی کا سلوک کیا جاتا تھا۔ یونان مصر اور یورپ میں غلاموں اور کنیزوں کو انسان نہیں سمجھا جاتا تھا، قانون بنانے، انتظام کرنے، تجارت کرنے، تعلیم حاصل کرنے غرض زندگی کے ہر شعبہ میں اونچ نیچ اور ناانصافی کا دور دورہ تھا۔ سیاسی حقوق چند لوگوں، خاندانوں یا گروہوں کو حاصل تھے۔ مگر اب حالات پورے طور پر بدل چکے ہیں۔ ہر طرف قانونی مساوات، اور سیاسی برابری پر زور دیا جارہا ہے۔

انسانی حقوق کے تحفظ اور ان کا فائدہ سب تک پہنچانے کا تشفی بخش انتظام ہر سطح پر موجود ہے اور دنیا کی تمام عورتوں اور مردوں کے لئے قانون میں نسل، جنس، مذہب، سماجی، سیاسی، معاشی، تعلیمی اور ثقافتی دائروں میں مکمل مساوات کا نظریہ تسلیم کرلیا گیا ہے۔ اس سلسلہ میں دنیا کے بڑے مذہبوں اور سیاسی و قانونی مفکرین نے بڑا کام کیا ہے۔ پھر بھی مساوات پسند سوسائٹی کو پوری دنیا میں فعّال اور چاق و چوبند بنانے کی ضرورت ہے۔

باب پنجم

کئی زبانوں والا ملک : ہمارا ہندوستان

پروفیسر امتیاز حسنین

دنیا کے زیادہ تر ملکوں میں ایک سے زائد زبانیں بولی جاتی ہیں۔ اندازہ ہے کہ اس وقت کرہ ارض کے 200 ملکوں میں 6000 زبانوں سے لوگ اپنی روزمرہ زندگی کا کام چلاتے ہیں۔ جہاں صرف ایک ہی زبان کا چلن ہے وہاں بھی ذائقہ بدلنے کے لئے علاقائی بولیوں کا سہارا لینا پڑتا ہے۔ زیادہ زبانوں والے ملکوں میں بہت سے لوگوں کی مادری زبان بھی ایک سے زیادہ ہوتی ہیں۔

دو زبانوں یا ان سے بھی زائد زبانوں کے استعمال نے افراد اور سماج دونوں کو مختلف طریقہ سے متاثر کیا ہے۔ جب کوئی شخص ایک یا اس سے زائد زبانیں بولتا اور سمجھتا ہے تو یہ سوال پیدا ہوتا ہے کہ یہ زبانیں اس نے کیسے اور کب سیکھیں؟ کیا اس نے بچپن میں یا اس کے بعد سیکھیں، ان کے اثرات اس پر کیا پڑے اور بولنے لکھنے پڑھنے میں اسے کیا فائدہ پہنچا؟ اسی طرح کسی سماج یا سوسائٹی میں دو یا زائد زبانوں کا درجہ، استعمال، مقبولیت اور ان کے مذہبی و معاشرتی اثرات بھی خاصی اہمیت رکھتے ہیں۔

دنیا کے زیادہ تر ملکوں میں کئی زبانوں کا استعمال اور رواج دو طریقوں سے ہوا۔ یا تو ان ملکوں میں یہ زبانیں علاقائی بنیاد پر موجود تھیں اور انہیں مرکزی سطح پر تسلیم کر

لیا گیا، مثلاً کناڈا۔ یہ ضروری نہیں کہ اس ملک میں ہر شخص ایک سے زائد زبانیں بولتا یا جانتا ہو۔ انیسویں صدی بلکہ بیسویں صدی کے شروع تک یہ سمجھا جاتا تھا کہ دو زبانوں یا اس سے زائد کا استعمال غیر اخلاقی، نامعتبر اور خرچیلا ہے اور عقلی بنیاد پر ان کو رد کر دیا جاتا ہے۔ بیسویں صدی کے آخر تک اس قسم کا منفی رویہ رکھنے میں سے روپرٹ مرڈوک جیسے نامور شخص نے ہندوستان میں ایک سے زیادہ زبانوں کے وجود اور استعمال کی مذمت کرتے ہوئے یہاں تک کہہ ڈالا کہ ''ہندوستان کی نا اتفاقی اور پسماندگی کی اصل وجہ یہی زبانوں کی کثرت ہے جب کہ اس کے مقابلہ میں انگریزی بولنے والی آبادی خوب متحد اور ترقی یافتہ ہے''۔ حیرت کی بات ہے کہ نشر و اشاعت کے میدان کے ایسے نامور اور اہم شخص نے ایک ملک ایک زبان کے جارحانہ نعرہ کو دہرایا اور اس تلخ حقیقت کو بالکل بھلا دیا کہ یہ غیر منصفانہ رویہ ملکی اور غیر ملکی لسانی اقلیتوں کے لئے بڑا تکلیف دہ اور غلط ہوگا۔

لیکن اب یہ منفی رجحان تیزی سے بدل رہا ہے اور دو یا اس سے بھی زائد زبانوں کی مقبولیت میں اضافہ ہو رہا ہے اور اسکے سیاسی اور تعلیمی فوائد کا اعتراف کھل کر کیا جا رہا ہے۔ زبانوں کی تحقیق اور ان کے دوررس تمدنی اور فکری اثرات میں مہذب و متمدن دنیا بڑی دلچسپی لے رہی ہے۔ کسی بھی ملک یا علاقہ میں افراد اور جماعتوں کے درمیان ذریعہ ابلاغ بڑی اہمیت رکھتا ہے خاص کر ہندوستان جیسے ملک میں جہاں متعدد مذاہب، کلچر اور رسم و رواج کے معتقد رہتے ہیں وہاں ایک دوسرے تک بات پہنچانے اور ان کے حالات سے واقفیت کے لئے ضروری ہے کہ یہاں لوگ ایک سے زیادہ

زبانوں کو استعمال کریں۔ اسی طریقہ سے ملک کے اتحاد، طاقت وانصاف کے توازن اور سماجی برابری کو برقرار رکھا جا سکتا ہے۔ اور اس ماحول میں کوئی خاص گروہ یا زبان اتنی طاقتور نہیں ہوسکتی کہ دوسروں کو ہر طرح دبا کر اپنا ماتحت رکھے۔ لسانی عصبیت اور زیادتی کے واقعات ہمیں تاریخ بتاتی ہے جو ہندوستان اور دنیا کے دوسرے ملکوں میں اس وقت پیش آئے جب برسر اقتدار گروہ نے اقلیت میں ہونے کے باوجود اپنی زبان سیکھنے پر دوسرے گروہوں کو مجبور کیا اور یہ بہت کم دیکھنے میں آیا کہ کمزور طبقوں کی زبان کو صاحب اقتدار لوگوں نے خوشی سے سیکھنا قبول کی۔ مثلاً فن لینڈ میں ڈچ اور سوئیڈ باشندوں کو زبردستی فن لینڈ کی زبان سیکھنا پڑی جب کہ خود فن لینڈ کے باشندوں نے ان کی زبانوں کو توجہ کے قابل نہیں سمجھا۔

ہندوستان میں ان گنت مذہبی فرقے، زبانیں، رسم الخط اور مختلف نسل و رنگت والے لوگ صدیوں سے ساتھ ساتھ رہ رہے ہیں۔ ہندو دھرم، بدھ اور جین مت اور سکھ ازم اسی سرزمین سے نکلے، باہر سے آنے والے مذہبوں میں اسلام، عیسائیت، یہودیت اور مزوکیت قابل ذکر ہیں۔ ان کے علاوہ ملک میں نہ معلوم کتنے قبائلی مذاہب اور عقیدوں کے ماننے والے لوگ رہتے ہیں۔ یہاں کے لسانی نقشہ پر انڈو آرین، ڈراویڈین، آسٹرو ایشیا ٹک، تبتّ و برمن اور انڈمانی زبانوں کے خاندان نظر آتے ہیں۔ بظاہر یہ بات انوکھی نظر آتی ہے کہ ہندوستان کی متحدہ قومیت اور مخلوط کلچر کے باوجود سینکڑوں سال سے زبان و بیان کے یہ اختلافات اپنی روایات کے ساتھ باقی اور تابندہ ہیں۔ اسکی تائید مردم شماری کے ریکارڈ اور سماجی وعلم لسانیات کے عالموں کی

ریسرچ سے ہوتی ہے۔ انگریزی دور حکومت میں سر جارج گریس نے ہندوستان کا لسانی جائزہ 1898 میں کر کے ایک مفصل رپورٹ تیار کی تھی۔

یہ بات دلچسپی سے خالی نہیں ہے کہ موجودہ ہندوستان کی زبانوں میں سے اکثریت کے رسم الخط برہمی رسم الخط سے نکلے ہیں۔ جسکا اولیں نمونہ تیسری صدی قبل مسیح اشوک کے زمانہ کے کتبوں میں ملتا ہے، اسکے بعد ہند وعہد میں رسم الخط کے دو نمونے کچھ تبدیلیوں کے ساتھ شمالی ہند اور جنوبی ہند میں رائج ہوئے، شمالی رسم الخط میں چوتھی پانچویں عیسوی صدی میں شاردا، لنڈا، گرمکھی، ٹکری کتیلا رسم الخط پیدا ہوئے، اسکے بعد کیتھی، مودی، رسم الخط آئے اور اس کے بعد ناگری رسم الخط وجود میں آیا۔ جنوبی ہندوستان میں برہمی رسم الخط سے کنڑا، تیلگو، تامل، ملیالم زبانوں کے رسم الخط نکلے، اسکے بعد ہندوستان میں عرب کے کوفی اور نسخ رسم الخط مسلمانوں کے ساتھ آئے۔ ہمارے دستور میں جن زبانوں کو تسلیم کیا گیا ان کی شناخت ان کے رسم الخط سے کی جاتی ہے ان کے علاوہ رومن خط بھی استعمال میں ہے۔

یہ واقعہ ہے کہ ہندوستان اور یہاں کے سماج کی اہم خصوصیت یہ رہی ہے کہ یہاں کئی زبانیں ہر زمانہ میں رائج رہیں، خاص کر مؤرخین کے مطابق انڈو آرین ڈراویڈین، آسٹرک اور سائنو تبتن زبانوں کا استعمال صدیوں سے ہوتا آرہا ہے۔ اس سے پتہ چلتا ہے کہ ہندوستان لسانی اعتبار سے دیو پیکر قد و قامت رکھتا ہے، یہاں زبانوں کی کثرت کا مفہوم دو الگ الگ طریقوں سے کیا جاتا ہے، ایک تو یہ کچھ خاص زبانوں کو اہمیت کی بنا پر سرکاری درجہ دیا گیا ہے اور باقی زبانیں عملی طور پر یہاں کے

باشندے اپنے اپنے علاقوں میں استعمال کرتے ہیں۔ 1991 کی مردم شماری سے پتہ چلا کہ ہندوستان میں 1576 مادری زبانیں موجود ہیں ، ہمارے دستور نے 22 زبانوں کو قومی زبان تسلیم کیا ہے، ساہتیہ اکیڈمی نے یہ درجہ 24 زبانوں کو دیا ہے۔ جبکہ آل انڈیا ریڈیو سے براڈ کاسٹ 80 زبانوں میں ہوتا ہے۔ زبانوں کی اس کثرت نے ملک کی تہذیبی رنگارنگی اور ایک دوسرے کو سمجھنے سمجھانے کا بڑا اچھا موقعہ فراہم کیا ہے۔ قومی رابطہ کے لئے ہندوستانی زبان بنی ہے جو دوسری زبانوں کے الفاظ کی وجہ سے کھچڑی کی طرح ہے جسے ملک کے زیادہ تر لوگ سمجھتے ہیں۔ یہ مسرت اور فخر کی بات ہے کہ ہمارے ملک کی سب ہی زبانوں کو اپنے دائرہ میں بڑھنے اور ترقی کرنے کا موقعہ حاصل ہے ان میں کوئی ٹکراؤ نظر نہیں آتا۔

ان زبانوں سے ہر طرح کی معلومات اور ضروری باتیں ملک کے طول وعرض میں بسنے والوں کو فراہم کی جاسکتی ہیں۔ زبانوں کی کثرت اور تنوع سے ذرائع ابلاغ، تعلیم، تفریح، تحقیق کے دائروں میں بڑی وسعت اور ہمہ گیری پیدا ہوگئی ہے جو کوئی معمولی بات نہیں۔

زبانوں کی کثرت اب ہمارے سماج اور ملک کی ایک قابل ذکر خصوصیت بن چکی ہے اسلئے ضروری ہے کہ اس اہم مفید وسیلہ سے پورا فائدہ اٹھایا جائے اور بلا ضرورت ملک کی زبانوں میں ایک دوسرے سے مقابلہ یا تنازعہ کی نوبت نہ آنے دی جائے۔ یہ کام ہمارے دانشوروں، انتظامیہ، مقنّنہ عدلیہ، سماجی کارکنوں اور میڈیا کا ہے۔ یہ اچھی طرح سمجھ لینا چاہیے کہ زبانوں کی کثرت نے بہت سی تعلیمی ، لسانی ، سیاسی

اور معاشی الجھنیں بھی پیدا کی ہیں جن کو انسانی فہم اور دماغ کی مدد سے حل کیا جاسکتا ہے۔ مثال کے طور پر انگریزی زبان کو پیش کیا جاسکتا ہے جو اس وقت دنیا کی متعدد زبانوں کو فروغ دینے کا اہم کام انجام دے رہی ہے۔ یہاں تک کہ اس سلسلہ میں لاطینی اور سنسکرت کا بھی نام لیا جاسکتا ہے جن کا شمار مردہ یا نیم مردہ زبانوں میں کیا جاتا ہے۔

لسانی اور علمی حیثیت کے تجربوں اور مطالعوں سے یہ پتہ چلا ہے کہ ایک زبان سیکھنے والے طالب علموں کے مقابلہ میں کئی زبانیں سیکھنے والے طلبہ نے اچھی صلاحیت اور لیاقت کا مظاہرہ کیا اور انہوں نے زیادہ نمبر حاصل کئے۔ ان لڑکوں نے لفظوں کی آواز، معنی نام اور تفصیل جلد سیکھ لی۔ اس طرح یہ کہا جاسکتا ہے کہ ایک سے زیادہ زبانیں سیکھنے والے طلبہ کی کارکردگی ایک زبان کے سیکھنے والوں سے کہیں بہتر ہوتی ہے۔

آخر میں اس بات کی طرف بھی توجہ دلانا ضروری ہے کہ دو زبانوں کی سرکاری سرپرستی اور مدد کی پالیسی جو ہمارے آئین کے مطابق ملک میں جاری ہے اس کے تحت ہندی اور انگریزی کو علاقائی زبانوں کے مقابلہ میں جو یک طرفہ ترجیح دی جارہی ہے، وہ ملک کی علاقائی زبانوں کے ارتقا اور فلاح کے لئے مضر ہے۔ اور اس سے ملک کی لسانی اور ثقافتی ترقی پر اچھا اثر نہیں مرتب ہوگا۔ اس لئے دانشوروں اور ملک چلانے والوں کو اس بارے میں غور کرکے سب ہی زبانوں کو پھلنے پھولنے اور بڑھنے کا موقعہ دینا چاہیے تاکہ ملک میں اندرونی خلفشار نہ پھیلے اور اسکا اتحاد قائم رہے۔